Holding On When Your Ladder Breaks

Holding On When Your Ladder Breaks

Coping With Crisis

Jodi Peters

© 2006 Photo by Photosmiths
Oakfield, New York 14125

Holding On When Your Ladder Breaks
Copyright © 2006 by Jodi Peters
All Rights Reserved.
No part of this book may be reproduced in any form, except for the inclusion of brief quotations in a review, without permission in writing from the author or publisher.

Unless otherwise noted, Scripture quotations are from the New International Version. The Committee on Bible Translation, June 1978 (Revised August 1983). Names of the translators and editors may be secured from the International Bible Society, translation sponsors of the New International Version, P.O. Box 62970, Colorado Springs, Colorado 80962-2970 U.S.A.

E-mail: crownassociates@bluefrog.com

Library of Congress Control Number: 2006928085
Library of Congress Cataloging-in-Publication Data
Holding On When Your Ladder Breaks

ISBN: 1-59330-391-2

Acknowledgements

I want to dedicate this book to our family, friends, and church in appreciation for all the support they have given to us in our time of struggles. We would not have made it through without their support and guidance. To our moms and dads: Ken and Sue, Terry and Ginny, Carl and Kathy, and grandparents for always being concerned and making sure we always had what we needed, but mostly for the spiritual guidance that has been our anchor. Uncle Dave and Aunt Pam, thanks for the support and the computer that enabled me to write! A special thanks to a great English teacher and friend, Mr. Motts, for your guidance and constructive criticism in this project. Lynn Wheeler, thank you for helping me to see the positive side of overwhelming circumstances. Our church family carried us in their prayers, thank you. Brenda, thanks for all the times you took care of the kids. Deb and Greg, for being great teachers to us and for showing us those leadership qualities. All our brothers and sisters, Rob, Chris, Andy, Nicky and Donald, Matt and Michelle, Tammy and Terry, and Pam and DJ thank you for your support and for the times you cared for the children, especially Pam for your English skills and advice, and Evan for believing in my dream and for telling me sometimes you have to take a risk to make them happen. Danelle and Jocelyn, for lending your ear to hear me whine, yet you always listened and prayed, thanks for your friendship. Brennan, Devon, and Alex, thanks for helping mommy and daddy when daddy didn't feel good, and for being good about letting me spend time putting together this book. To baby Collin, God told me that you were going to be a sign of healing, of peace, and of faith. Mom, Dad, and Russ, you told me I could do it, and because you told me, I had faith. Mom you were my lifeline on the phone. Russ, you are the love of my life, thanks for sticking with me through the tough times. My desire is that those who read this will find the hope, the peace, and the healing that they are looking for.

Table of Contents

PART ONE: For Better or Worse

I'll Love You Forever	3
In Sickness and In Health	31
New House, New Baby	43
Waiting, Praying, Hoping For a Miracle	57
The Monster Inside	71
No More Monsters Just Darkness	87

PART TWO: Using Your Tools

A Gerbil In a Spinning Wheel	99
Being a Tool and Using Your Tools	103
Treading On Serpents and Scorpions	107
"I Can Conquer the World"	127
The Exodus	135
The Lifeless Shoes	143
In His Own Words	147

Forward

When the winds blow, when the waves come crashing in around us, we must hold steadfast to the anchor in our life, Jesus Christ. For He knows all, He sees all, and He has power over all things. He is the Lighthouse in the storm and His light shines gently calling us to come into His loving arms. When we have nowhere else to turn, His arms are opened wide. Run to Him, cleave to Him, and hold onto Him with all your strength.

To my beautiful family whom I would never trade the world for. Things may not have always been peaceful, and there may have been a few moments from time to time that were not happy or that we would like to forget. But we have lived a great life and will continue to do so despite the misfortunes that come against us. We will ride out the storms together no matter how hard the boat rocks. If the water begins to fill the boat, we will bail until the boat is dry again. And if the Lord walks to us upon the water, we will without fear muster all the confidence needed to walk with Him hand in hand and not sink into the depths of the threatening waters.

I have done my best to make each of you feel secure in all that we have been facing. That to me is still not good enough. I will make it my priority in life to make sure that my "best" is never quite good enough, for then I will never become complacent in my efforts to serve you, and to love you all in the way you deserve.

The title, *Holding On When Your Ladder Breaks* came about as part of a vision I received one day. I have always had the desire to write. Anybody that knows me has heard me joke and say, "Before I die, I want to write a book." As Russ and I began to face the difficulties caused by his back injuries, little did I know that my dream would begin to flourish. Romantic dates for Russ and I consisted of hour long drives with three car sick children in and out of Rochester every week, only to face the uncertainties of clinics, and procedures. I always looked into the clouds and prayed that God would give me enough strength to get through just that day. One day as I prayed I seemed to see a crude ladder, the kind more common in Bible times reaching to the Heavens. I kept this vision to myself, but began to see it every time we took those discouraging drives. Each time I would hear the title and see a person hanging from this ladder with all the rungs breaking out beneath him.

Time moved on and I began putting some thoughts down on paper, always filled with doubt that a book would ever really develop. A new member of our church knew of our situation but did not know any specifics and definitely knew nothing of my desire to write a book. She gave me a card of encouragement and I was taken back by the picture on the front of the card. It was a crude ladder just like the one God had been showing me in the sky. That was a confirmation to me that the book was a go, so by blind faith, a multitude of struggles, and a lot of hard work it has come to be. The project which God began combined with my life long dream was finally a reality.

Part One
Φ
For Better or Worse

Chapter One

I'll Love You Forever...

All of my life I dreamed of marrying him. I could not concentrate on anything else, each day I was consumed with making him notice me. His love songs wooed me, and the sound of his voice made me feel so light I felt as if I could walk on air.

He was striking and he took my breath away. I was not just drawn to him because of his blonde hair, blue eyes, or the strength in his forearms, the broad shoulders, or the cut in his upper body, but mostly to his smile that would whirl my stomach into somersaults. Not only was he tender, but he could take my heartache and fix it without saying a word. All I needed him to do was to look straight through me, and I knew I would be safe.

We shared the same passions in life. We loved to have fun, and when we dated, we loved to dream about our future together, like what kind of cars we would drive, how many children we would have, and what their names would be. We even drew a sketch of what our home would look like, and even tried to decide on what kind of dog we wanted. Russ even talked about his dream to go "big time" in the music ministry, and wondered how that would affect our relationship if it were to happen, especially if we were to start a family. The love of music was a strong chord in itself that kept us strung together. Life's experiences moved us to write and create our own songs that would not only heal our troubled hearts, but would also reach others who were searching to deepen their faith in God, or for others perhaps to find God for the first time.

Our love was not about knowing that we would make a great couple because we went together like hand and glove, and it was not about marrying the one we could live with for the rest of our lives, instead, for both of us, it was about marrying the one we could not live without. That was our fate, we were destined to be a couple and my life long dream to marry Russ and have a family became official on August 20, 1988. Neither one of us would have any clue as to the forks and turns we would encounter along the road, as well as the disability that would strike my husband ten years down the road.

    I had first laid eyes on Russ when I was only about eight years old. What would I, an eight year old have known about love? Yet I found myself trying to put myself in the right place at the right time just to be near him. He was easy to make smile, and I had found that being around him made me feel warm and fuzzy. Obviously, at that young stage in my life I was not looking to date, or to have him send me roses, or to write me a poem, or to even call me on the phone. I did, however, desire to be near him, and to have him as a friend. Could it have been God back then steering my heart towards this young man who would one day become my husband? I would have to think so. Why else would this young man captivate me and consume my every thought for years to come and still there after the point of saying, "I do"?

    We remained very close friends growing up and even had innocent experiences where he had kissed me and later only to break my heart. Russ and I shared the same church and youth group, sang in the same gospel groups, and even shared the same sect of friends. There was no escaping the fact that outside of school, we saw a lot of each other. If that had not been enough, the older I grew the more my love for him grew as well.

    We dated other people, but still held a torch for one another. There was a void that only he could fill in me, and dating others only made that void bigger, and made my heart ache for him even more. I felt we were the man and woman in a love story that were passionate for one another, waiting and longing to come together, only to have circumstances always drive them apart. Every time circumstances kept us apart, it only made our fondness for one another grow stronger, and the strong friendship we had would in turn be the foundation that would keep our love secure for the future that awaited us.

Through my teen years, I was the rebound after his breakups. Always hoping the next time that he would come to me would be for a real, lasting relationship. Did he not even consider me to be human? Whenever his relationships would end, he would come to me, and then leave again. It was near impossible to be free from my feelings for him because any relationship he had with others would share the same school, church or youth group. Before I had won his affections, my heart had been broken beyond repair. It was tired of waiting for his heart to find me as more than a friend. I wanted his heart for a lifetime, not for a moment in time. I found myself praying again as I had done for so many years before, that God would make him my husband. I swore to the Lord that if He would only allow my dream to come true, that I would not neglect my first love, which was Him. In the meantime, I tried hard to forget Russ and began focusing on serving the Lord. I had actually become so frustrated with him, that it started turning into a love-hate relationship. If I could not have things my way, it would be no way at all, and the very sight of him began to repulse me. I was old fashioned, meek and mild, and to confront him about the way that I felt seemed too forward to me, besides the fact that he was committed to another relationship.

I began to date other guys, tired of waiting for him to come to his senses. I began to witness something unusual. Whenever my boyfriend would be with all of us, Russ and his girlfriend always had problems. Russ noticed that someone else was paying attention to me. I thought it was hilarious. I knew for sure when this became a familiar pattern, that Russ really did have feelings for me. At the time that I became serious about my boyfriend, he shared with me that he had joined the Air Force a couple of weeks before we had met.

All I had to show for my relationship once my boyfriend left each time was his ring around my neck, never realizing though how important his ring around my neck would be in showing my future husband, Russ, how faithful I could be in a relationship. Little did I know was that Russ was watching me while my boyfriend was away, to see if the mouse would play. Russ was left with a lot of insecurities in his life after his parents' break up years before. He was unable to trust in his relationships, afraid of being hurt again. Right before the letters in the mail began slowing down for me, Russ's relationship was on the brink once again.

Somehow something seemed different about him. He seemed more in tune with God, his priorities were straight, and he seemed to be more mature in all aspects of the word. After realizing according to Russ, that his girlfriend at the time was not who he wanted to spend the rest of his life with, he returned the engagement ring he had purchased and reflected upon a different ring he had seen hanging around my neck with the word faithfulness engraved all over it. Even though I was not his for the taking, he sat patiently, and waited to see what I would do.

Each day I ran to the mail box or waited by the phone. I sent packages and post cards across the sea, wondering why my love had stopped doting on me. I began to flounder like a fish out of water with thoughts for Russ again. One, because weeks went by and I had no clue if I even had a boyfriend anymore, and two, because ironically Russ was available to date, and was acting very interested in me. Finally, it happened, the letter had arrived at the end of my junior year of high school. My boyfriend rambled on about how I deserved someone better than him, and in a nutshell, decided to call off our relationship. Not making sense to me at all, I did wonder if it was all God working things out. He never came out and said, "I don't think we should see each other anymore, or why don't we just play the field until

I come home from England." I did not know what to make of this letter I received.

I remembered being angry at the world! I hated Russ for hurting me in the past, but also did not want to lose him forever. Now I hated my boyfriend for doing this to me when he was so far away from home, and for leaving me clueless as to what he was really trying to say to me. I totally surrendered to God. I remembered saying, "God, I can't take this anymore! Please help me...I will serve you no matter what, but right now everywhere I serve I'm surrounded by Russ. He's not in a relationship now, and now I'm being dumped! Do you want us together or what?" All the times I had dated, my true fondness always turned toward Russ. Now I was totally confused as to what was going on in my life. I just wanted to run away where I did not know anyone and where no one knew the people I was running from. I had for the first time really felt alone.

My boyfriend and I broke up that day. It was official; I was free after being so faithful for two years only to be crushed in the end. Was there anything I could possibly learn from that whole experience? Ironically, Russ called me about a youth meeting that we were both supposed to attend, and I took that time to share with him what had happened to me. He said, "Jo, I know exactly how you feel." He called me Jo. Like we were best friends, and listened to me about my lost love. It was strange, and I listened to him about what happened in his break up. That night, my mother and I were cooking in the kitchen when I shared with her that Russ was going to be at the same youth training meeting that night. She jokingly said, "Wouldn't it be something if you guys ended up getting married?" Repulsed I replied, "Not in this lifetime, I am so over him!"

Russ and I attended the meeting that our youth counselors held for anyone who had a desire to work with the youth in the future. Their goal was to train young adults in the youth ministry, the funny part was, that Russ and I had been the only youth who responded, and therefore were the only young adults there that night. I remembered feeling strange, because it was no secret to our youth counselors that we held a torch for one another. There was also no secret in the fact that Russ was now very much available to date just as I was. I found myself on the outside acting unresponsive to his gestures, but inside screaming with excitement. I remembered thinking, "Girl, you've got it bad. You ain't over him. What is wrong with you?" I decided to play hard to get. I had to leave the meeting earlier than he did, so I said goodbye to everyone and made my quick exit, hoping to leave behind some mystery as to why I was leaving so early. Maybe somehow it would make him curious and cause him to chase after me. As I started my car, I could have sworn that I had heard him shout my name. Inside I heard a little voice say, "Okay, now you are hearing things that aren't even there! Just put him out of your head." Then I heard it again. "Jo," he shouted. As I began to shut my door he leaned into the window and asked if I would like to go to the movies sometime. Inside I kept saying, "Pinch me, pinch me, I must be dreaming!" Instantly, though thrilled as I was, I had remembered the many times it had led to this only to have my heart broken once too many times.

A wall went up immediately. I saw red flags, and danger signs everywhere. The funny thing about it was I had not started driving my car yet! Then a thought struck me. If he was available now, and things could be truly different for us, then there was no harm in playing hard to get. So, I decided to string him along like I felt he had done to me for years. To his invitation I replied, "Ahh, I don't know…I'll think about it." I tried to act as uninterested as I could. A part of me wanted to hurt him back for all the pain I had felt from his many rejections. Yet a part of me still felt or knew that he would be the only thing that would bring out the real me again.

Every song I heard on the radio reminded me of him because he was here; I could see him. My ex-boyfriend on the other hand, was hard to envision because I had gone so long without seeing him. The lovey-dovey side of me heard songs like Bryan Adams's, *"...Everything I do, I do it for you...there's no love, like your love, and no other could give more love. There's no where, unless you're there, all the time, all the way..."* The love-hate side of me heard songs like Pat Benetar's, *"...You're a heartbreaker, dream-maker, love-taken don't you mess around with me..."* The harder I tried to get Russ out of my head, the more he appeared before me. Was this a sign? Was I missing something?

I was getting ready for my senior year of high school, and suddenly I was faced with, what will I do? What does God want me to do with my life? Should I just move away to college somewhere and forget this life that keeps centering on this guy? The next couple of months spent seeking God brought peace to my mind. My mother had always told me that God was not a God of confusion, but a God of order and of peace. Russ and I attended more youth training meetings, and our counselors were willing to let us work behind the scenes with the teens. This meant that Russ and I would have times when we would be able to present a teaching to them. Sometimes it meant helping to plan outings, major events and retreats. Even though we were not a couple, the Lord knew what He was doing. We both began working in the Youth Ministry. The strong ties we had in music, youth work, and the way we viewed life in general kept us intertwined even when circumstances would not allow us to come together.

In the summer of 1987, my heart would never beat the same. Trying to escape a family quarrel, I stopped into our church where some of us would be having band practice. Russ and his best buddy were the only ones there. I remembered feeling quite uncomfortable. I was crying and quite broken. Russ suggested that the three of us pray for my situation, and we did. Russ was very concerned, and did not like to see me upset. After I regained my composure, I left for home to see how things with my family were. I had not been home for long when the phone rang. Russ was calling to see how I was and informed me that the band would be going out for pizza. He wanted to know if I wanted to go along. Before I knew it there I was going for pizza with the man of my dreams!

He was very tender, and very concerned as to how I was doing emotionally. Everything I needed from him, everything I wanted, I felt were being communicated to me that night. All night long I was teased with thoughts of us being a couple. My feelings for him came alive once again. As we would get in and out of the car, the summer breeze would catch his cologne and carry it to my nostrils, it was just the right bait to reel me in. The way he looked at me that night was quite different. I knew immediately that something was not the same. I realized that Russ had finally *really* noticed me. No longer was he admiring my qualities, and characteristics, this time, he was seeing me in a way he had never seen me before.

As my mind began to become involved with him again, he began to take on chivalrous natures. He paid for my food, he opened doors, and he was sincere in every way. Then the time approached ever too quickly. It was time to call it a night. I had no idea that the night would just begin. It would be a night I would never forget. Russ made sure that his friend would take the others home, that way we would be able to be alone. As we got into his car, I became very nervous. I was now beginning to sweat the very moment I had been waiting for, *the kiss.* He had kissed me before but it was always when he was confused about his life and when he was supposedly dating others, so it never felt right. This night would be different; it would be just the two of us, no strings attached.

The windows were rolled down, and the wind whistled through the car. Every time we had come to a stop the bullfrogs and crickets could be heard singing their lullaby, a perfect symphony, for a seemingly romantic night. They seemed to keep time with the beating of my heart. On the drive home it was obvious to me that he was not taking the direct route to my house, which told me that he probably was going to want to talk. He pulled off the side of the road. The stars shimmered in the evening sky, and the moon caste silhouettes everywhere. "Wow, it's beautiful with everything lit up," he said as he got out and walked to the front of the car. "Can you smell the fresh air? It's gorgeous out," I said as I walked to the front of the car as well. Before I could blink, he grabbed a hold of my jean jacket and pulled me close to kiss me.

I could have cried a river from the amount of things that melted in me at that moment. Although I did not, I was overcome with such joy that I was moved to tears. Something inside told me that this time would be different. God, I believe, had orchestrated our lives up to that night when we came together. This was His timing, and it was our time to experience what true love in Christ was meant to feel like. My stomach flip flopped with excitement, and I remembered wanting to stay lost in that moment forever. I could tell that his heart was beating as hard as mine, and I knew that he was trying to be my Knight in Shining Armor. What he did not realize was that it was not going to take anything special to convince me that he was good enough for me. He could have been Dr. Jeckyl or Mr. Hyde, and I would have been just as determined to be with him!

We talked for hours that night in my driveway. My mother was less than thrilled. Inside I think she was just as ecstatic as I was. She was probably thinking, "I won't have to listen to her cry the blues about him anymore!" I do not think that I slept a wink that night. So many thoughts raced through my mind. I was constantly threatened by our on again off again rebound relationship from the past, that my mind would become paralyzed with fear. Then part of me would see him differently, and I hoped and prayed that I was not setting myself up for a fall.

For the longest time in our relationship, I was extremely cautious. The trust had to be earned in my eyes. He had no reasons not to trust me; however I had every reason to mistrust him. If he messed up with me, there were not going to be any second chances.

After a couple of months of dating, and a few serious discussions with one another, I really began to see a different side of this man that I loved. I saw someone who had matured a lot since our breakups. Russ also loved the Lord, and desired to serve Him with his music. Because Russ loved the Lord, and had a daily relationship with Him, this set him apart from most guys. I also had a daily relationship with the Lord. We had a common bond, one of wanting to spread the gospel through working with teens and our music. Our relationship would prove to be different from most of our peers because of the intimacy of the Lord in our lives. Not only did our walks with the Lord blossom, but so did our relationship together. I like to believe that because Russ and I put God first in our lives as young teens, and concentrated on serving Him, that God answered our dreams and placed our lives together.

Russ showed up after work at his usual time, and as time went on, we knew that we belonged with each other. We were both called into the Youth Ministry as well as to music, therefore having known one another our whole lives; we decided to get married that next year. Our parents were concerned that we were too young and not prepared for the world yet. We did not want to wait. Soon into our courting, we began making wedding plans. Our dates consisted of going to the movies, youth functions, and dinner. Many times we just hung out at my house, content in just being together. We did not have to be doing something spectacular to have fun and to feel close to one another. Music was always involved in our relationship somehow. There were times we would go for a walk on a trail, and Russ would stop and play a song that he had written for me. Coming from a guy, who unlike a girl, would not choose to talk about his feelings, I must say it was spectacular! His feelings spoke louder in a song versus a two hour conversation.

Not too long after we had been dating, Russ had to go to New Jersey for training on his job. We felt ripped apart when he had to leave. It was for approximately four or five days. We had been so used to seeing one another everyday, it was tearing us apart just to think that we would be separated for even a short amount of time. The day came when it was time for him to leave. A tearing took place in my heart. He left me with his car to use which was awesome considering I did not have one of my own. It also made me feel close to him. As the days went by without him near, my mind began wondering what life would be like without him now. He was able to call a couple of times, to let me know that he was alright, but whenever I went to bed at night, I would have to play some of my favorite Chicago tunes which was a mistake because it only caused me to long for him even more. Still to this day, those Chicago tunes have a special spot in my heart.

"...Saturday in the Park, I think it was the Fourth of July... You're the meaning in my life, you're the inspiration, you bring feeling to my life, you're the inspiration, I want to have you near me, I wanna have you hear me saying..." I would also spray his cologne on my pillow so as to smell him near.

Russ was due to arrive home on a school night around nine o'clock. I waited and watched all night. Finally I saw the headlights pull into the driveway. His boss was dropping him off so he could pick up his car. The welcome home kiss was greater than the night we started dating. I never wanted to feel that separation again. There were no lavish gifts, and no souvenirs, yet a beautiful love song emerged from being apart.

> "So Far Away" (from you)
> Tonight, while I lie awake in bed
> So far away from you,
> My heart, it breaks from all the pain
> I feel inside without you.
> But baby I can feel your love right here
> I feel in my heart and through my tears
> Oh baby, I love you
> I love you.
> Loves may come and go,
> But either way I know
> That you're mine, all mine.
> And we know not what the future holds,
> But sooner or later, His plan will unfold.
> And I, through the words of this simple song,
> Will try to explain just how I feel,
> That baby if you'll stay with me forever,
> Then we can build a family together.
> Oh baby, I love you, I love you.
> And baby if you'll stay with me forever,
> Then we can build a family together.
> Oh baby, I love you, I love you.
> So baby, "What do ya say, let's find a way?"

We decided that we needed to start making some type of plans since we would have less than a year before we would become man and wife. Russ's dad began building a house at the back of their trailer and once upon completion, he would be looking to sell the trailer. We saw it as a great opportunity for us to have a home! Russ and I shared our thoughts with all of our parents. Sometimes they would seem fine with everything, but most of the time everyone seemed concerned that we were just not ready for this. This made us upset, yet determined to show them that we were responsible, and serious. So we continued our plans. Our parents guided us and showed us how to create a sample budget. We asked our parents what they paid on utilities, gas, food, and other expenses. They gave us figures from their experience to get us brain storming.

Russ had a job at a state facility working as a supervisor for the mentally challenged. My father was quite concerned whether Russ would be able to provide for me, and was concerned that there were no opportunities for advancement there. My mother and father had married young as well and had a family immediately. Although they had no regrets, they knew the struggles of not having enough money, having children to feed, and no opportunities for better paying jobs. My father was just trying to have the best for me, yet at the time his deep issue with my future husband furthering his education and finding a better paying job before we were to be married, was upsetting Russ very much. This put me in an awkward position. I was torn between the two men that I loved. I could see both of their points. Russ was upset if I wanted to listen to my father and my daddy was feeling replaced by the new man in my life. Once things became stressed in all of our relationships, it was hard to make things normal once again.

After work each day Russ would stop to see me. I'm sure that my parents did not appreciate someone else always being around for supper, distracting me when I had homework to be done, or keeping them up late on the weekends. Mom and dad never said a word. I believe that my mother knew before Russ and I came together that we would be married one day. My mother kept working on my father. Dad would always be near a window watching for my safe, prompt return from a night out with this new man invading his territory. If we were one minute late, he would pace the floors without saying a word, and scratch his ear (a habit he had when he was upset or nervous). All of the children in our house as well as our dates learned quickly to read how dad was feeling by watching his actions.

Since I was in my senior year of school, I was going to be extremely busy as were my fellow classmates, except the fact that I would also be having bridal showers, and a wedding to be ready for two months after graduation. My life was already becoming quite different from the lives of my friends. I found myself clinging more to Russ.

The first major event of my senior year would be the Jr. Miss Program. There were only two of us that would represent our school. My mother and I were ecstatic! I think in some ways my mother was so excited and supportive in the things I chose to do because she never had the opportunities that I had, and she would have desired to do the things in much the same way as I. Maybe in some ways I would be fulfilling dreams that she would have had. Or maybe they were simply just the dreams she had for her daughter coming true. There would be sixteen representatives. Two girls from every high school in the county would be representing their school.

When we had our first practice we were told that the judge's interview would count as 50% of each girl's score. This would prove to be the most crucial part of the program. Each girl would have approximately fifteen minutes with approximately five or more judges to answer important issues on politics, religion, and on life in general. This interview would take place the afternoon of the program. We were also told of all the other categories and what their value of scoring would mean. The one that stood out the most to me was the talent. Our instructor said that we would need to pick some type of talent such as singing, dancing, or the playing of some type of an instrument. Some girls were quite nervous. They would continue to approach our instructor and say, "I don't do any of those things. What am I going to do?" The instructor would then make an announcement to calm fears and explain that they could do a drama or poetry as well. Still for those whom these things did not come easy to, this would prove to be the area in which they would struggle. For me, on the other hand, this would be my strength, and I would make it my time to shine!

God had truly blessed me in the area of music. I was already used to performing in front of many people because of the bands that I had played in. I could play the piano and sing, and had no difficulties in doing both at the same time. Immediately, the wheels began to turn inside my head, and that first day I knew exactly what I was going to do. I could hardly wait to share it with my mother! As I came home from practice I spelled it all out to my mother. I explained to her that everything in our talent had to be completely put together on our own. That meant that costumes would have to be home-made, and music would have to be played or recorded by ourselves. She said, "Well, what is it that you want to do?" "I'm going to be Fieval the mouse, from *The American Tail*," I said.

The American Tail was a new movie that had just been released that year. It was a story of a mouse that had become separated from his family. During the movie the young mouse sings a song as he dreams of being reunited with them. The song became a number one hit on the radio, and I knew it would captivate everyone. I felt if I dressed up as the mouse, and sang the hit song, that I would have a very good chance of winning.

The pressure was on! It would prove not to be a small feat. My mother began the makings of the greatest mouse costume in the world! I purchased the sheet music for the song, and began playing it over and over until I knew it like the back of my hand. I was also on the search to find out what the other girls had decided to do for their talent. Some were playing piano, doing a dance, putting together a drama, and quite of few would be singing. I began to become fretful. How would I be able to stand out from the others that were singing or playing the piano? Then I had an idea that no one else would be able to do. Another love of mine was to experiment with sign language. I imagined myself in a mouse costume that was home-made, singing and signing to a, pre-recorded tape with me playing the theme song, *"Somewhere Out There"* on the piano. This would be a sensation! It would also be exactly what the judges were looking for by having each contestant do as much of the creating, and work themselves.

As I was busy planning and attending rehearsals for the Program, Russ was busy telling me fibs that he was working late. His plan was to sneak up to the jewelry store to pick up our rings. He had taken me shopping weeks before, wanting to ensure that I had the exact diamond I had always dreamed of. While looking for what seemed like forever through *"gaudy"* the *"way too elaborate"* the, *"wouldn't look right on me"* rings, I finally discovered the one that took my breath away! Everyone that knows me knows how much I love the snow, and the holidays that come along with the winter season. My diamond was set in what looked like a snowflake setting, perfectly centered between the six points. The good news was that we could get his and her matching bands all in a set.

The days were growing cold, but not our love for one another. Russ wanted to take me to the piece of land he had purchased for us. More than four and a half acres of property with a wooded, creek down in back; the view was just breathtaking. I could not understand his urgency to take me there, especially when we had not eaten supper yet, but I knew he felt the need to have me there, so away we went. Since there was not a driveway already existing, we would pull in what was then, a field. "Let's take a walk down to the creek," he said. Even though it was chilly, and the walk back from the creek would be an uphill climb, I said, "Okay." The whole time I wondered why on this cold day before supper, he would feel such urgency to visit where we were going to make our home. I loved visiting it too, and dreaming of what our life together would be like there. We also tried to picture a real driveway, and our trailer! This particular day, the day after Thanksgiving, Russ seemed to have something more pressing drawing us there.

We prayed and thanked God for how he was working in our lives as we made our way down to the creek. Russ must have been planning for days how to ask me to marry him, because it was just a day I will never forget. By the time that we had reached the bottom of the green meadow, the chilly air released its magic. Light, fluffy flakes falling ever so gently, disappearing as soon as they fell on our hair; it was the perfect moment to pop the question, and he seized the opportunity. "Jo," he said as he pulled my snowflake diamond out of his pocket and grabbed my hand. "Will you marry me?" he asked. Of course, I said, "Yes!" I struggled to see him place my snowflake diamond on my finger because of the snowflakes that were falling on my eyelashes, so I just let myself get caught up in the moment, and I began to cry. He chuckled and pulled me in close for a hug, "I love you Jo, and I want to spend the rest of my life with you." We were engaged now, and nothing could get in our way.

Everything was in place, the stage was set, the Jr. Miss Program was about to begin. I remembered being a basket case that morning. The judge's interview was the part all of us had been dreading. My mother dropped me off at the school where the program would be held. She saw the fear in my eyes when I heard the other girls talking about some of the kinds of questions that the judges would be asking each girl individually within the next few moments. I heard a few of them saying, "deficit". I had no clue what that was, and fretfully began to ask my mother what in the world it was. My mother tried to explain, however it was of no use, my mind was not able to comprehend anything because it was so ridden with fear. Instead of trying to get a crash course on politics before the interview, I decided to pray and ask God to give me the ability to understand and answer the necessary questions.

I remembered something my piano teacher's sister relayed on to me when she realized I was one of the contestants. She apparently had some head knowledge of how the judge's interview was conducted. Her words of wisdom to me were, "Be confident in your answers. They do not score you well if your answers are inconsistent with your convictions." For example, if I were to say that I was Pro-Life, and then they asked me if I felt that a woman had the right to choose to have an abortion, they would look to see the consistency with my answers and convictions. They would not judge me on whether my answers were right or wrong in their eyes. I had determined in my mind that, that was what I was going to do. Be frank, and be honest with them, and if I did not understand a question like, the "deficit", then I would say so.

I was up next for the interview. My knees were knocking, but I felt the peace of the Lord. One of the first questions that they threw at me was, "If there was an accident involving an older gentleman, and a woman who was pregnant and you could only help to save one of them, which one would you choose?" With confidence I said, "I would choose the pregnant woman because she is carrying another life within her, therefore I would be saving two lives. The older gentleman has also had more years to live his life." This was consistent with my Pro- Life conviction. Just when I thought everything was going well they asked who I would vote for in the upcoming Presidential Election. That was the year that Pat Robertson was running for the Presidency. I remembered becoming fretful immediately, wondering where that question would lead. Then with confidence I said, "Well, by now, I think we all know that answer, Pat Robertson!" Everyone chuckled, since they obviously had, a pretty clear view of my religious/political views.

The interview was over, and all we needed to worry about was looking and performing our best. It seemed like days as I sat back stage and waited my turn. Being number fifteen for everything in the program was frustrating because I had time on my hands to fret about what was to come, and second guess the things that I had already completed. The time came, and I heard the Master of Ceremonies introducing me as Fieval, the mouse from *The American Tail*. Fieval's wiry tail and floppy ears made everyone whisper and chuckle before I even began. Before I knew it, I was done, and it was a sensation just as I had planned. Not one mistake and people stood and cheered, and Russ whistled, hooted, and howled my name, however my close friends were missing and that hurt me deeply. The rest was in the hands of our judges. As the night came to a close, all sixteen of us, stood holding onto hands just like you would see on the Miss America Pageant. I really felt inside that I had a chance at winning the Talent, but really did not feel I would walk away with anything. The winners of the different categories were being named and so far my name had not been called, and then I heard the MC naming what the recipient of the talent category would win, and then I heard, "And the winner of the talent category is number fifteen, Miss Jodi Gibson!" I could not believe I had actually pulled it off. All of those months of hard work and practice. Before I knew it I was being hugged and kissed by all the other girls, and walking arm in arm with a gentleman that would take me to receive my award. I went into the Program telling the Lord that I would be content in just finishing in fourth place. I had no intentions in competing in any more competitions down the road and therefore I would feel content and satisfied with a small win. Four girls were going to be picked. They would also receive some nice scholarship money, and modeling opportunities.

"Our fourth runner up goes to, number fifteen, Miss Jodi Gibson!" Fourth place was just what I told the Lord I would be happy with! I was awestruck, and overwhelmed with strong feelings of joy, pride, satisfaction and relief. I immediately realized that I must have scored very high with the judges to have been placed in the top four. What stunned me however, was the fact that I was the only young lady who was not involved in the Honor Society, or that had outstanding academic records. From the beginning, I had felt like a fish out of water knowing that my achievements academically did not measure up to the others involved in the Program. I had really felt that the judges would favor those who excelled and had received honors in areas previously. Therefore in my eyes, I did not stand a chance! Afterwards, several pictures were taken with family and my new Jr. Miss friends. Finally after arriving home exhausted, I wanted to go straight to my room to get out of my gown and into something more comfortable. My mom and Russ knew that would be my plan and therefore, had my room decorated with balloons and streamers!

The first major event of my senior year was completed. Now with less than eight months before the wedding, Russ and I had to focus more on our plans. The dream that every girl waits to plan with her friends and family was happening. Russ was left with issues in his own life since his parents' break up when he was a child. He became a very angry, bitter man who held onto a lot of unforgiveness. He grew up as most children, feeling that somehow the divorce was his fault. Confusion about relationships, trust, and women troubled him deeply, and as the time came closer to our wedding date, he began to share in detail about what the divorce had done to him. He shared things with me that he had never confided in anyone else before. One of the honors I suppose from showing my faithfulness to him and to the Lord. He knew he could truly trust me when he realized that I too, would walk his road of pain with him.

We began pre-marital counseling sessions to find out who we were as individuals, and to find out what each other expected or anticipated about sharing our lives together. We never anticipated any problems, and never dreamed we would encounter the, "sickness and in health" part of our vows. Now that I look back at our innocence, I have come to realize that most people are ignorant at what the marriage vow is really saying. Most are oblivious as to the seriousness of the vow taken, and spend their lives living to fulfill dreams and are never prepared for the twist and turns that can bend a relationship out of shape.

I remembered our last meeting with the pastor, who was also my father-in-law. Russ's dad wanted to make sure I knew that Russ had some concerns about marriage, one, wanting to make double sure that his marriage did not end up in a divorce as well. Even though I won Russ's heart because I displayed characteristics he had admired and been looking for in a girl, he had been burned before, and had never been loved with a pure and genuine love free from jealousies, and manipulations. In his mind he felt, "I like this, but can I trust it?"

I remembered feeling angry the day we sat in his father's office talking about how I would need to understand what Russ felt. He had been a product of divorce and wanted to make sure that would not happen in our marriage. Instead, I felt like saying, "Hey guys, I'm the one who's marrying the man that dumped me how many times only to use me again on the rebound. Not only do I have trust issues because I'm actually marrying the one who hurt me, but the friendships I had for years were now strained because of the choice he had made in me. Who should need who to understand concerns? It should be you guys understanding my concerns or hurts!" All the focus centered on Russ's insecurities that I had no part in at all. But somehow I felt I was being punished for the mistakes that others made in his life. Yet because I loved him, I sat there and kept my mouth shut, and never shared *my* real feelings.

We wanted our wedding to be unique. I wanted to have all of the girls in red. It was breathtaking when we finally saw the red dresses against the white tuxes. The white seemed to scream the words clean and pure, a symbolism of our love for Christ and one another. I had decided to carry a single white rose in an open Precious Moments Bible, versus carrying a full bouquet of flowers. The girls would carry single red roses. The guys were in white tuxes to match the groom. As far as getting carried away in incredible detail from the photography to the honeymoon, we kept things simple. There were no bridal registries back then, and no elaborate gifts received. My mother and father kept the cost of the wedding to themselves except for the cost of my gown which I found on sale for @ $400.00. We planned to have a dessert reception for everyone that was invited to the wedding and a nice sit down meal for those in the wedding party as well as immediate family. There was no band, or traditional bouquet and garter throwing. Since it was a tradition to keep the wedding dress a secret from the prospecting husband to be, Russ grew increasingly concerned whether or not I would reveal a little too much of myself. The only thing I had fretted was how Russ would kiss me in front of all of those people the day we were joined together. I wanted a peck on the cheek or lips.

My dream since I was a little girl was beginning to unfold. I had loved him and prayed to marry him since I was in grade school. So in spite of his imperfections and insecurities, I was really living the life I wanted. My wedding was bitter sweet; I was filled with many emotions. I had always had a great relationship with my parents, so my last night at home was traumatic for all of us. My sister had come home to spend the night since she had already moved out on her own. Mom and I had spent the day putting my things in boxes. Special memories being hurriedly packed away without time to reminisce, it almost felt as if I was throwing away the first part of my life and starting a new one. In a way that is true when you leave home and get married, but all of a sudden it was upon me and I felt as if the child in me would be lost forever. There were tears and a few laughs as well as serious talks about becoming a wife as well as a lover to my husband to be. My mother and I could always talk about intimate issues as uncomfortable as they are at times, she did not send me out to the wolves.

I remembered driving by what would become my new home, and saw Russ and his little brother carrying in some of Russ's things, and it finally hit me. All the pieces to my dream life were being put together slowly one piece at a time. By that time the next day I would no longer be Jodi Sue Gibson, but Mrs. Russell Peters. Everything seemed fairy tallish. Were we too young, too immature; were we ready to spend the rest of our lives together? What would my relationship be like with my family, his family, and my friendships once I say I do? There were so many questions that I did not have the answers to. Mostly in my mind was, "Would I be loved the same by everyone that was apart of my life?"

It was heart wrenching to leave my family because my life was my family and Russ even though I loved him dearly, had broken my heart once too many times, and he was the one I would spend the rest of my life with. My mom and I were close, and I wanted to be like her in every way. She told me I could do anything, and was such a big supporter of anything I did, but mostly she poured into me life in Christ and taught me how to behave as a Christian young woman, and used her motherly instincts to guide and shape me and to discern what was best for me. The two of us could watch movies together and cry and laugh at the same parts. I even shared the same love of horses as she.

My dad and I were close as well. It would be very hard to leave my daddy, because daddies make everything all better for their little girls when things just do not go as planned. When the spider dangles in the corner, he is the Super Hero that rescues her and gets rid of the bad guy. He is the one who holds her in his strong arms when she is too scared to try something new or is afraid that danger is close by. Her daddy is the one she will believe when he tells her that she is a pretty little girl, or a beautiful young woman, because if daddy sees it, then her husband will too. Daddies are the head of the house, and have the final say in their children's rights for mercy or judgment, and along with that come a respect and a reverent fear to honor him just as we should honor God.

Even though it is hard for mommies to let go, I think when they know their daughter is marrying the man of her dreams, they share in that joy and fulfillment from remembering themselves, what it was like when their Knight in Shining Armor came riding into the picture. On the other hand, daddies are losing their innocent little girl to another man. Another man that will touch her, love her, make a family with her, and cause her heart to be captivated with his love, and before you know it daddies begin to feel their little girl slip away. I saw the pain in my dad's face when Russ asked for my hand in marriage. I saw him get choked up, and I'm not certain but it is possible there was even a tear in his eye. He was quiet, and was concerned that I would be hurt by Russ once again. My dad wanted so much to protect me from love wronging me as it had in the past, but he loved me so much that he took a chance to let me go to something I had longed for, for so long. It is the same way with our relationship with God. He lets us go to the things we chase after. God will warn us just as our earthly father will of the consequences of our actions, and then He lets us go because of our own free will and hopes and prays we make the right choices. I thank God for giving me a godly father who still to this day guides, advises, comforts, and loves me and my little family.

    I did not sleep a wink that last night at home. I was too worried about not hearing the alarm clock, or worried that I would put a run in my stockings. Before I knew it, I was at the church getting into my wedding dress. Everyone and everything was arriving at the church, from the groom to the flowers and the cake to the pianist, all was well at 1:00P.M. The wedding was to start at 3:30 P.M. My piano teacher would start playing her selections at 2:30 while everyone was being seated. I wondered if Russ was nervous. Did guys get nervous about these kinds of things? I remembered not being nervous, just uptight, and worried about everything being properly placed or running smoothly.

I heard the music playing and imagined all the people being ushered to their seats.

"Oh my gosh! Where are my vows?" I asked to all who were in the bridal room.

"Calm down, they have to be here somewhere. We'll find them," my mother reassured me.

I had written my vows to Russ a couple of nights before, and tried to have them memorized, however, it was imperative to me to have it in hand just in case. Now they were gone! I started to panic. I pictured myself stuttering and stammering all over the place!

"I Jodi take you..." is all I could remember.

"Come on! God please help me to remember, bring it back to me," I prayed.

Immediately I felt flushed with fear. This is not the way it is supposed to be. Everything is supposed to be perfect. I started getting agitated with the flower girl and ring bearer, and anyone else that asked me a stupid question. To make matters worse, the photographer was taking little cutesy pictures before the wedding started! My whole life flashed before me because I could not remember the vows, and it was being captured on film! I never did find my vows; I clearly walked down the isle in faith that God would move me to speak something similar to what I had.

The last song to be played before I was to be at the back of the foyer doors was, "*My Tribute*" arranged by Dino Kartsonakis. It had been my last recital piece, and had been a very challenging piece to perform. I thought it would be special if my piano teacher of thirteen years would play my final recital piece. After the wedding, my video would reveal that the piece had been quite the success even though I had been unable to see it for myself. The piece starts out in the very beginning with a gliss. At the end of the gliss, the music has reached its maximum volume. Every head turned and began to stare at my piano teacher. Some mouths were even hanging on the floor in shock and amazement that a song could be so dramatic and beautiful all in the same.

The *"Bridal Chorus"* began to play, and I locked arms with my father. Then I saw him. After all of the groomsmen took their places, there was Russ, and he was looking at me longingly. I saw the serious look on Russ's face and I started to shake. My father felt my Bible starting to shake and said, "Here," and he placed his hand under mine to keep my Bible from shaking. It was a tender moment I wanted to treasure forever. Another funny moment captured on video was that my father was so nervous he chewed gum all the way down the isle. I was too nervous to notice when it was actually happening, but that is another good reason why you should video tape your wedding.

I tried to get a quick look around to assess that everything was in its proper place, but once I saw everyone looking at me and admiring my dress, my lip began to quiver. I quickly took refuge in the only other place to draw comfort from; that someone else I knew was feeling exactly like me, my future husband. I knew when I looked into his eyes, that we were doing the right thing, and that we were ready. When my father and I approached the altar, Russ was quick to want to take my hand. I remembered being upset a little bit because I felt torn between the two. I felt like Russ was going to have me forever, but this was the last time my dad would be that close to me. How can one be filled with so many emotions at once?

Russ was going to present his vows to me first. I was relieved. I was desperate now, and thought possibly I could get back on track with my vows by hearing him get started. He pulled out his guitar that had been strategically placed off to the side where I could not see it. Surprise! He had put his vows into a song for me. What I did not find out until later was that he had written the song the night before. The song was the perfect wedding song, unlike anything that Adam Sandler would sing in the movie, *The Wedding Singer.*

The kiss was not the peck on the lips I was hoping for; instead he kissed me good, hard and long. I remembered being embarrassed at first, but it was sealed, over and done with. Our lives we felt would be perfect forever but what we did not count on was what would happen a few years down the road that would send our "merry-go-round" world spinning out of control. "For better for worse, for richer or poorer, in sickness and in health, I do…"

Chapter Two

In Sickness and In Health...

"Bye babe, I love you," he said before he walked out of the door for work.

The smell of his cologne made my stomach turn over with the joy I felt when we were first in love. He always kissed my lips gently three times before we parted. His kisses always made me feel like we had a "secret code" with one another, no matter what demanded our time at that moment the "secret code" would never be broken.

"Love you too," I mumbled as I snuggled under the warm blankets; thankful that I was not the breadwinner of the family having to wake to the roar of the alarm at 3:30 a.m.

I never fully fell back asleep after Russ walked out of the door partly because I found myself praying that God would keep him safe as we were apart for the day and that He would bring him safely home again. It may have seemed strange to some, but my heart ached for him even though we were not oceans apart. I was love struck and that was all there was to it. Family would tell us, "Give it a while, the honeymoon will wear off in time." I could not help but to think, "What is wrong with these people? They sure must be miserable in their marriages!" We had been married approximately ten years by then and the honeymoon was still exciting!

The child within kicked and reminded me of the countless blessings that God had bestowed upon us since the time Russ and I first came together. Not only was our third child on the way, but Russ and I were madly in love; had been blessed with a beautiful family, a new home, a good paying job, and a life rich in spiritual blessings.

I heard the familiar sound of Devon's feet hitting the floor. This child was a built in alarm clock for me. It never failed, he could be put to bed at 1:00 a.m., and still rise with the sun. Devon required very little sleep and never ran on empty. I, on the other hand, turned into a monster when I did not receive my beauty rest. As much as we loved each other, the two of us were night and day. I do admit that I loved it when my children crawled into bed with me once their father left. Devon's visits in our room were short lived only because he expected a three course meal as soon as he jumped onto my bed and insisted on fixing it himself if I did not abide by his time schedule. This of course would be no small feat for a three year old. So naturally I dragged myself out of my warm bed to keep peace and order in the kitchen. I was not always the happy camper. Brennan on the other hand would sleep until noon if I'd let him.

Whenever I was expecting a child my body was overcome with fatigue for the first trimester. All I wanted was to sleep. In order for me to sleep meant that my children would need to sleep and that was a chore in itself. Brennan was eight and I was his school teacher since we chose to home school our children. In a strange way, Devon taught me time management, forcing me to become motivated, and he also showed me how to make the most of my time. Not only was there school to be taught, but I had an active three year old under my feet, and music students in my home by evening. This left only a hurried time for any kind of rest for my body and the growing child within.

The kids and I listened for the sound of dad's work truck backing down the driveway at noon most days of the week. They quickly learned that, "Beep, beep, beep," was dad's truck as it rolled backwards down the driveway.

"Daddy, daddy!" they shouted as they ran to his truck. I could hear the sound of Russ throwing open the latch on his truck allowing the back doors to swing open. Then I would hear him say, "There are my boys! How's your day so far?" Then he would hop down off the back of the truck to lift the kids up to the stash of goodies that were stored inside. Candy bars, little snack bags, or a can of pop were among the choices of the day. After dad picked out a sandwich for himself, we would all head inside to share a quick, but very enjoyable lunch together. I remembered I could never hide how glad I was to see him. For both of us it helped to break up the day and sustained us until he would be home for the night. I always dreaded the last swallow of his sandwich because it was hard to see him leave.

A workday for Russ was not nine to five. His hours were from 4:45 a.m. until 5:00 or 5:30 p.m. He would leave the house at 3:30 a.m. and not arrive back home until 6:00 p.m. Russ was dead tired before he walked through the door. I was amazed how he would never let it show to the children. Instead, he would let them jump and tackle him before he could take his boots off.

"Okay, okay, guys; that's enough! Daddy's back is hurting a little bit," he said.

Russ had been seeing a chiropractor for two months to see if a few adjustments would correct pressure he had been feeling in his upper back, which also caused him to have trouble breathing. Russ was strong and I did not worry too much. We figured a few adjustments would fix him up and that he would be back to himself in no time. I never imagined what would follow.

After supper we took our usual stroll around the yard in the cool of the evening, looking at the growth on our newly planted shrubbery. We finally had our home that was sketched out ten years before. The kids looked forward to this time of the day where they could show off for both mom and dad at the same time. We could not help but reminisce to the time when we had dreamed about what we were living at that very moment. A new home positioned just so on our property, garnished with landscaping to our fancy, beautiful children who were healthy, and a love in our marriage that never seemed to struggle. We had a picture perfect life.

"Ugh!" Russ said as we were walking in the backyard.
"What's wrong?" I asked.

He was hunched over holding onto his back.

"I can't explain it Jo, it feels like my spine is slipping," he said.

"What do you mean?"

"It has happened a few times recently. I'll be walking along, and I can feel something slip, I'm scared Jo, it feels like my spine. I notice whenever I walk on uneven ground something gives and I swear I feel something slip back there!"

Now I began to worry. He was scaring me, and I did not know what to do because whenever I was scared he was the one to comfort me, and now it was reversed. We were both scared, yet he was helpless, and for the first time I felt lost in our marriage.

"That's it! You're not going to work tomorrow. So call somebody right now, and tell them you will not be in for a couple of days."

"Jodi, how can I do that? I can't miss any work."

"Russ, you can't even walk. How the heck are you going to run your route? I'm calling the doctor in the morning. I don't like the sounds of this!"

Russ took three days off to see the chiropractor again and told the doctor that his upper back and breathing seemed to have improved, however, the problem seemed to relocate itself in the low back. He told him how he felt like something was slipping, and how uncomfortable it was to walk. The chiropractor ordered a thoracic x-ray upon which he found nothing. We then went to see our primary physician who ordered a complete set of x-rays of the back. Initial examinations concluded nothing, allowing Russ to feel that everyone thought he was over exaggerating. I found myself having to drive us everywhere because he was so uncomfortable, yet I myself was having great difficulty fitting behind the steering wheel in that stage of the pregnancy. However, it was difficult to see him in such discomfort; so I tried to look beyond my discomfort still feeling completely helpless for Russ. Those three days off of work rolled over into a long weekend; in which we thanked God for. We seriously thought that the extra days off of work would rest his back enough so that he could return on Monday.

Being the problem solver that I am, I remembered flooding him with questions.

"Russ, do you remember doing anything to your back?"

I needed answers to stop the worry I felt inside.

"There was an incident on my truck the other day. It was very strange. I was pulling food off of the shelves for an order at one of my accounts, when suddenly it felt as if my truck had been bumped by something. Immediately I fell backwards against the shelf and within seconds everything seemed to be spinning. This all happened so quickly yet it seemed to be in slow motion all in the same. I remembered thinking 'What in the world was that?' I got up and went to see if anything had hit the truck. There was absolutely nothing around the truck at all. Later on is when the nagging pain started in my back, and I began to get concerned as to how I would be able to finish my job."

"Did you tell work what happened?"

I remembered crying because at the time I was more emotional due to the pregnancy. I was overcome with great fear. I just could not hold it in anymore.

"We've got a baby on the way, what are we going to do? What if you can't go back? What's going to happen to us?"

He lifted my chin and our lips were sealed with our "secret code".

"Jo, all I know is that the Lord will provide."

As we were lying in bed that night, the voices of those who said, "Give it time the honeymoon will wear off eventually," echoed in my mind. I also remembered the word that was given to us the day of our wedding. "…No matter what hard times you face, you will always have each other to hold through the night." I found myself drawing comfort in what that word truly meant.

All of a sudden it hit me that our road was about to get bumpy and I did not know if we were ready for the ride. That night he let me cry myself to sleep on his chest...I still felt safe there.

The birds were singing a lullaby and the sun danced across my face as I lay there still wrapped in Russ's arms. I knew that soon we would hear the pitter- patter of little feet. I did not want to leave the safety of his arms, but the bigger my stomach got the more uncomfortable it was to lie there. I got out of bed and peaked at the children. I loved to watch them sleep. They had no worries at all, except with what toy they would play with that day, or for the spider that was dangling in the corner of their room. The boys both had blonde hair and blue eyes just like the two of us; however, they took on the features of their father's side of the family. They were both sleeping so peacefully; they had no clue of the uncertainties we faced ahead. Their tummies would rise and fall as they took in a much, needed rest from the romping they had done the day before.

Despite the discomfort of Russ's back, we were all enjoying that daddy was at home with us for a while. The children were elated that dad had all this time for them now, and that he could see what our days at home had been like when he had been gone at work. Russ loved being with us, and didn't mind having some time off from work, however, I had seen how restless he had become. Russ was never one to sit still, and now I began to see exactly whom our three year old received that trait from. Not only did Russ work sixty hour weeks, but after a full day and weather permitting, he would have the yard and vehicle maintenance, ministries in and outside of church, and the roles of husband and father to fulfill. He would always be fixing things, writing music, and just on the go with something. You would never see him sitting around with time on his hands. Now the table was turned. Not only did he have a lot of time on his hands, he was finding great difficulty in doing simple things such as bending over to tie his shoes or brushing his teeth, walking, sitting or standing too long, and definitely anything that involved lifting, running, throwing, bending, twisting. Basically, he had difficulty with every day tasks.

Our follow up appointment with our primary physician could not come quick enough. The not knowing what was going on was killing us. Yet, on the other hand, we were scared to death to find out the results of the x-rays. Our doctor pointed to the x-rays and showed us exactly where the problem was. He told us that Russ had a broken vertebra which could only be corrected by surgery.

"Your spine is slipping forward, and catching. You are right in what you have been feeling all along."

What a comfort to know that they had found something. Not that we wanted anything to be wrong with him. There were times in the beginning, when we felt like the doctors did not believe us, because they could not find anything at first. Now in a sort of weird way, we felt justified. There was documented proof that something was causing him to feel this way, we were not nuts. "I want you to see this neurosurgeon. He's out of Rochester, and he's the best." What our doctor did not tell us was that it would take months of waiting to even see this doctor. We did not realize that this was just the beginning of a nightmare from hell.

We began to inform our loved ones as well as church family of our devastating news. We were terribly frightened, and needed to reach out for support. They gave generously with love, money, prayers and babysitting. God was our lifeline and still is today. God's word had proven true time and again; He is the same yesterday, today, and forever. Our faith took a roller coaster ride, and although we felt everything around us changing, God never moved, never let us drown in the waters, and never let us burn in the fire.

Two weeks had passed since Russ had been to work. His place of employment was more than generous to us. The corporation covered our health insurance 100%, and we started receiving Worker's Compensation benefits. Before our first Compensation check rolled in we expected one final regular pay-check. As uncomfortable as we felt with Russ not at work for a time, we still needed that paycheck and therefore decided to load the two boys in the car and make picking up that check a family outing. The boys argued and aggravated one another as usual and Russ and I realized this was far from a joy ride. Tensions high, we pulled into the parking lot and decided to let daddy go in to pick up the check while I waited with the ever impatient boys. I thought that I would be ahead of the game by taking those few seconds to make out a quick grocery list, and inform the two in the back seat of our surprise to take them to Burger King.

The boys swung their legs with joy and squealed as daddy approached the vehicle.

"Give me your check," I said.

"There isn't one."

"Quit joking. I need to sign your name and make out the deposit slip. Hurry up, now where is it, Peters!"

"Jo, I'm not joking. We won't be getting one this week!"

"What are you talking about, no paycheck. How does that happen?"

"This paycheck is actually going to be paying me for unused sick and personal days, and... I don't know...I don't understand all the reasons why...but that's it...no check. It's going to be awhile before we get it."

"Boys, knock it off! Are you going to tell them or should I?"

"What are you talking about? Tell who, what?"

"The boys! Tell them we can't afford to take them to Burger King now that we said we would!"

"No, we said we would take them and we will."

"Russ, do you realize the setback that will happen by missing just one paycheck?"

I'll never forget the look of fear in Russ's eyes when I began to cry and lose all hope. This bumpy road we were traveling down was beginning to shake us. Russ was a rock, a man of his word, and he soothed the pain of every grim circumstance when he said, "We're going to stop right now and pray, guys. God sees our situation, and He already knows our needs. He will take care of us."

With each day I grew bigger and bigger, yet so did my fear. I feared that we would not have health insurance by the time the baby arrived. I knew that the money saved in the bank would have to pay the new mortgage and take care of other responsibilities until our finances were set. Would they ever be now with a husband who might not be capable of working? My emotions were raw due to the pregnancy. Depression, anxiety, and the fear of the unknown were eating at my nerves. We wrestled with the decision of whether or not it would be right to go on our vacation I had previously planned. Colonial Williamsburg, and a place on Virginia Beach for two weeks was what we had been waiting and saving for. A stressed working, and home school mom, and a husband who worked more than sixty hours a week anticipated time away from the hustle and bustle of everyday life. Now with the added stress with Russ's back and a baby on the way, we really longed to get away; however, it just did not seem feasible. The hardest decision to cancel our reservations had proven to be the wisest down the road.

Russ's back was progressively getting worse, and trying to get a neurosurgeon to squeeze us in seemed light years away. Our primary care physician saw my husband as well as our chiropractor within the first couple of months of his injury. We did not see the neurosurgeon until July 10, 1998, three months later! The sitting and driving to and from Rochester for those appointments increased the pain and inflammation in his back. Many times we dragged two carsick children along. I never thought I would make it through. Kids were fighting; there was car sickness, a husband moaning in pain all the way, packed snacks and toys for the day, not to mention having to drive expressways in a busy city for the first time by myself.

I will never forget seeing this surgeon for the first time. He was a tall, strawberry blonde man in his early to mid forties. I remembered he spoke with such confidence and reassurance that he had seen cases such as my husband's before. I found myself putting my hopes into this man, maybe in a strange sort of a way hoping that he was an angel in disguise sent from God above to answer our prayers. I remembered him stating at that time that surgery was usually inevitable. The lowest vertebra (L-5) in Russ's back had been fractured. He felt that since my husband was so young that we should try less invasive ways of treatment before plunging head long into surgery. One less invasive treatment would be to play around with medicines, secondly to have an MRI done, and thirdly to be fitted for a back brace. "Would you like morning or afternoon," said the receptionist. Yes! I was so glad to finally be in that office making a second appointment. We were finally in with this guy, we were now one of his regulars and I have to tell you it felt wonderful! "Do you have late mornings?" I asked. "How about September 29th at 11:00?" I remembered thinking, "Is she for real? That's over two months from now. Doesn't she realize we will have a baby by then? Why are we scheduling an appointment that far from now?" I just did not understand and before I could think of what to say, out it came.

"Sure, that's fine."

Little did I know my timidity working with doctors, the system, and attorneys would cause me to grow in strength, wisdom, and a need to trust in a power that was stronger than any court system. After we made it home that day there were many calls to make. Loved ones waited anxiously for a report. Our family and friends were so supportive and offered to help in any way they could.

We kept silent about our finances due to embarrassment, and not wanting to humble ourselves in receiving handouts. Deep inside of me I wanted to run back home to my daddy. Just like when I would be sick, hurt, or scared when I was a little girl, my daddy made me feel safe. They did not have to even do anything but say, "You're going to be alright," and you just knew everything would be. I needed that reassurance more than ever. I never realized that all the times I did not run home to dad that my Heavenly Father longed for me to run into His arms for comfort. I knew the Lord was there, but I never fully realized the intimacy God wanted to show me. I could have run home, but I had a husband, two little boys sensing a change going on, and another child growing inside of me. This made me think past my own needs, and therefore I reached deeper within myself and found new strength to continue at least for another day.

Chapter Three

New House New Baby...

Everyone especially I was growing anxious to meet the little one I had carried for several months now. There was less room inside for the baby to grow and less room for mama to fit through the doorways. The arrival date was soon approaching. The baby's nursery was ready and completely done in white and pastels. I was more excited this time around due to the fact that it was the first baby in our new home.

I had more difficulties carrying this child than with any of the others. I had scoliosis (curvature of the spine) and the added weight and positioning of the baby inside caused painful back spasms which placed me right out on the floor. This was quite a sight since I could not lie on my back when I was having one, and there was definitely no way for me to lie on my big belly. Instead, I would moan and scream all the way down to the floor struggling to find a comfortable position. Usually I was sprawled out sideways or on all fours riding out the spasm. I had reached a breaking point and knew I could not last much longer. We all prayed that God would help me to go naturally. I had never needed any drugs or epidurals with my other labors. With my first, the doctor broke my water and labor began on its own. My labor was only eight hours long. My second delivery consisted of an experimental gel to jump start labor because I was two weeks overdue and began to fill up with fluid. The doctor induced at 7:00 P.M. and said, "See ya at about 7:00 in the morning." I remembered thinking, "What, twelve hours, is he nuts?" In four hours the baby arrived. Somehow I knew the third would come much quicker. It was evident that God had always blessed my labors and deliveries.

On August the 18th at three o'clock in the morning, I awoke with uncomfortable contractions lasting every six minutes. Every mother feels mixed emotions about labor and delivery. Fear, excitement, pain, and relief that the end was near is what I remembered feeling. I continued in pain for three hours before waking my husband, who was at that time loaded up on painkillers, anti-inflammatories, and muscle relaxers. Needless to say, he did not wake easily. I found myself feeling selfish that I wanted him to comfort me while he was suffering in so much pain of his own.

The closer we got to the hospital the pain decreased, and my fear came true. I was having false labor. I remembered feeling so embarrassed that everyone had made such a fuss. Being my third time around you would think I would be able to tell the difference. My mother just smiled and said, "Well, you wanted to go naturally and now's not the time." My mother never made me feel like I was over reacting, being a baby, or was putting her out. I needed her so much.

Disappointed, we left to pick up the kids who would be disappointed as well when they saw there was no baby. Everyone fended for themselves for supper that night, mom had orders to rest. That is what I did. I kept to a very light dinner, not knowing if we would be visiting the hospital for real the next time. I remembered crying many times before about being fearful that I would have those horrible back spasms for labor since I had been having them so frequently.

I went to bed early for a change and could not believe it when I awoke with pain at three o'clock in the morning for a second night in a row. Three hours later I awoke my husband again, this time in excruciating pain. He began to pray for me that God would be merciful, and that I would find favor in His eyes and have another easy labor and delivery. I called the doctor and informed him that I felt this was it. I remembered telling him that the pain was intense this time and that it must be the real thing. He said, "Good, I mean not... well that you're in pain, but good because you wanted to go naturally and it looks as if you are. Why don't you head into the hospital in a while and have them page me, take care."

I had already determined that I would ride out as much of the labor at home as possible without cutting it too close in getting to the hospital. I did not want to be hooked up with monitors that would tell you when a contraction would come before I could even feel it. It scared me. I did not want the noise of nurses, monitors, or any poking before it was absolutely necessary. My brother Evan came up to the house to take care of our boys until my sister Pam could pick them up and keep them until the baby was delivered.

My husband walked me around the yard with his back brace on, in pain, and groggy from the medicines. He rubbed my back and told me everything would be fine. He helped me focus and count through the hardest contractions, as I grew frustrated with every other one. The contractions that came closer together were not as intense, but the ones that came further apart were unbearable. I was confused. Usually it worked that the closer together, the more intense all the way through till delivery. Mine were backwards therefore; I thought that it was not true labor.

As we approached the hospital I thought I felt the urge to push and I grew scared that we would not make it. I could just see the headlines! "Man in back brace delivers own child!" I always hated that they needed insurance information when you were in so much pain. A nurse came downstairs with a wheelchair to whiz me upstairs to have me checked. My doctor was paged and my husband was left filling out the paper work. My mother was called again and told that it was the real thing. I remembered feeling scared even though it was my third time around. I think the fact that there was already so much uncertainty in our lives with Russ's back coupled with the intense pain that it made me unsure if I could face this delivery even with my mom and husband by my side. I found myself worrying more about Russ and how he was going to be able to endure however long it took for this baby to arrive. He tried to disguise his pain, but when you live with someone for ten years, you learn to read your spouse like a book. Russ was munching while the doctor and he watched something on television waiting for my next response. I remembered feeling sick from the smell of Russ's food, and upset at the fact that the two of them made small talk when I was suffering. All true signs of a woman in serious labor!

Then it was time. The television went off due to my request, and the sandwich was set aside, the appointed day and time of our baby's arrival was here. Natural it was, and the desire to bring this child forth grew more intense. Our baby came out with her eyes opened as she looked curiously at the world surrounding her. It was a sight that my doctor had never seen. In fact, the doctor kept stating to everyone, "Will you look at this, look at her looking around; I've never seen anything like it!" So everyone stared at her in all her curiosity of the new place she was entering, that no one realized the sex of the baby. I was the one who looked and finally discovered I had received the little girl I had hoped for. The day before our ten-year anniversary made the perfect gift for both Russ and I and an excellent reminder that we would never forget our anniversary.

Alexandra Mae held captive the hearts of her admirers. She had soft brown hair with golden highlights. Everyone joked that her Aunt Tammy, our hair stylist, had already visited her with her potions and lotions. It was almost as if I was having my first baby all over again. I was so used to opening blue things, boy things; not little pink, frilly, girly things! I did not know how to change a little girl's diaper, or bath her. I was not even experienced in putting in little hair clips. Would I learn to distinguish the cries of my little girl as I did my little boys? Every time her little lip quivered or curled under to cry, it softened our hearts so much.

I always loved the smell of a new baby. I loved their need to need me. I felt their kicks and somersaults, and would even rub their bottoms or feet as they were growing inside of me. Therefore, they already knew me too, and I was the one they cried for in the night, I was the one they wanted when they needed to rock and nurse whenever their tummies urged them to cry. Babies learn the smell of their mothers as well. It does not matter how experienced someone is with babies, babies can smell and sense that it is not their mother and therefore send out a cry for her.

There was such amazement when she came home. Everything she would ever learn, say, or do would be different than the boys. We would just laugh when she would cry to nurse because it grew louder and stronger as if to say, "I demand that you come over here right now and feed me!" She would exaggerate much more than the boys in order to get what she wanted. I knew she was already trying to wrap daddy right around her little finger. What I questioned was did he?

I remembered bragging to everyone how great she slept that first week. We were a little concerned as to why she seemed so satisfied all the time. I did not remember the boys sleeping so much or being that content. My mother reassured me that I used to be the same way. After the first week however, Alex did a complete turn around. She became the most colicky baby on earth. Daytime, nighttime, she would not sleep. Her cries ate at my nerves. All of a sudden I went from having so much peace, and joy, to being the most miserable, selfish person in the world. I could not believe that this little creature could cause me to turn into such a monster!

A colicky baby, postpartum blues, and the stress of Russ's disability were causing me to lose control of my sanity. Russ was able to be at home all the time unlike when the boys were babies. He however, could not carry her, pick her up, or put her down. Changing diapers was difficult because he was constantly in a back brace, which limited what he could do. My husband was home, but it felt sometimes as if he were so far away. Between his pain fatiguing him, and medicines making him groggy or sick, it was hard for him to really be there for me, and I began to resent him for it.

I began to say horrible things such as, "I can't enjoy her! She's making me insane!" Russ would take her for me and try to calm both of us at the same time. I would have to walk away and cool off to try and see life through her eyes. Maybe something I was eating was upsetting her tummy. I would watch what I ate, try to burp her more often, and nothing changed the fact that I had a colicky baby who became very demanding of my time. I could not help but feel that everything was working against me. My husband broke his back and was facing major back surgery just before Christmas, I had a colicky baby, I never slept and it was now time to begin to school the boys for the new school year. Anger and self-pity became my companions.

It was soon time for Russ's second appointment at the surgeon's office. Two carsick children, a colicky baby, a drugged up husband and a partridge in a pear tree! We made our way to the heart of the city once again. Snacks, toys, diapers, wipes, and well, no bottles, you guessed it, I would have to nurse and time things just right! We had not even had school for a full month and I was already taking days off of school for Russ's doctor appointments, and that was just the beginning of a horrible nightmare. There was never anyone available to care for the kids, so it always became a family affair.

We waited, and waited, and waited...

"Boys, I told you to keep your hands to yourselves," I said bouncing a colicky baby. There was Russ walking and stretching because we had already been waiting approximately forty minutes.

"Come on, how much longer is it going to be," he whispered to me.

"I don't know, but she's going to have to nurse pretty soon," I said panicking.

"Russell Peters."

"Yep," he said as he began to approach the receptionist.

I remembered being angry at anything. It was everyone's fault for me being miserable. I started needing to blame everyone else for my bad attitude. Anything else that went wrong after that would be the receptionist's fault. It did not matter if it were my kids acting up, or if someone in front of me on the drive home was poking along and holding us up. She started everything off from the beginning, so I would just bad mouth her all day and all night, like somehow it would justify everything I was feeling.

The surgeon informed us that Russ would be set up for major back surgery on December 3, 1998. The back brace was not helping and was aggravating his back more. The medicines were doing little to help his pain. There was no way around it anymore. He had a problem, and it needed to be fixed as soon as possible. The surgeon would perform what was called Rays Cage Fusion. This was a newer type of fusion, which involved the removal of the disc that lain between the two lower vertebrae. Instead, in its place would be placed two titanium screws (cages), hollow inside and perforated on the outside. They would proceed by taking the piece of broken vertebra (L5) and crush it down in order to pack the hollow screws. This would give him a double fusion. Bone to metal, and as his crushed bone would begin to graph through the perforated cages, it would also be a bone to bone fusion.

The one thing I will never forget was how optimistic our surgeon was. "Oh yeh, he'll be able to return to work probably in a couple of months," he'd say. Russ would tell him he did not see how he would ever be able to do that job again, seeing as to how his back broke because of all the heavy lifting, bending, and twisting, he did year after year. Our surgeon never wanted to say that he could not ever work again, or maybe he should not return to that line of work. For two reasons, one being, Russ was thirty years old with his whole life ahead of him, secondly, our surgeon did not like handling compensation cases, in which we did not realize until we began needing his testimonies in court in order to win our disability case.

I remembered relief and fear hit me like a freight train when we were finally told that surgery was being scheduled. I was most afraid to lose Russ to a major complication. He had gone so far down hill with his back condition, and lost so much of his strength just in a matter months, so to me the biggest fear was ultimately losing him. At that point in our lives before the surgery, life seemed more fragile, and the rapid decline of my husband's health seemed like it would only lead to his death. When I was scared Russ was the one to offer comfort. The fear had a way of dissipating when he touched me. I would be left grief stricken when my husband would be too depressed or be in too much pain to ease my worries. I grieved deeply; and secretly for the man I loved to return. Not that I did not love Russ the way he was, but I did not recognize him anymore. Not only did Russ's life change through this, but our whole family as well. Nothing would ever be the same. Not our walks with God, our marriage, our family unit, and our relationships with family and friends would all be put to the test. I found myself longing for the old life like the Israelites when they wandered in the wilderness. How they longed for the days when they knew they would have a meal and a place to lay their head, even though they were in bondage. They were comfortable as long as they knew when they would eat, or where they would lie. Our life was easier and comfortable when Russ was strong and healthy, now we were being moved out of our comfort zones to a place we were unsure we wanted to go, but we held onto our faith and trusted God to lead us through. There were times that even though we had the support of family and friends, that we still felt alone or the outcasts of society. For instance, they were able to continue buying nice things, going to the movies or out for a nice dinner. They for the most part had their health, happiness, and were capable of bettering their future. It was hard not to be envious. Most of the time even though we had our faith it was our children that kept us going. If it had not been for three precious faces, I do not know if Russ and I would have survived in our marriage. The children were so helpless like children are. They solely depended upon us for everything. If they had sensed any insecurity with our situation, then it was up to us to make sure they felt secure and loved. How would we be able to do that if Russ and I did not work together as a team?

Russ and I decided to start praying together for a half an hour each night. We prayed for a miracle, financial needs to be met, and even for food. Most importantly we asked God for strength to endure however long it would take for our situation to pass. I remembered back to times earlier in our marriage when Russ would awaken in the night.

"Are you sick?" I asked.

"No," he would reply.

"If you're not sick, then what's wrong? Why can't you sleep?

"God's calling me, Jo. I've got to pray and spend some time in the Word."

"Are you sure you're alright?"

"I'll just be a little bit."

He kissed me in our secret code and walked away in the dark. I loved that I had such a godly man in my life. I quickly drifted off again…

Quite often I found him losing sleep because God was calling him to get up. It reminded me of great men in the Bible who had similar experiences. For instance, when Samuel was a small boy and stayed with Eli in the temple, he heard someone who he thought at the time was Eli calling him. This happened several times in the middle of the night. Repeatedly, Samuel would go to Eli's bedside and ask him what he wanted. Eli eventually wised up and realized that God was calling Samuel and told

Samuel how to respond the next time he heard the Lord calling his name. The next time the Lord called Samuel, he replied, "Yes, Lord. Here I am." The Lord proceeded to give Samuel a prophecy about Eli's family.

I found myself bewildered that God used men of today in the same way. I was proud to have a husband that was not a carouser. He never hung out with the guys in bars groping over women that would walk by. He loved his little family and strived at making sure that our household served the Lord. Russ never squelched my ideas, or kept me from having new friends of my own. He had always been where he said he would be, and always came home from work with a smile, and the jealousies and insecurities that were there before we married disappeared the day we became husband and wife. My husband was a man of his word. Faithfulness was his greatest attribute, but more so to this God we had never seen.

As we sat to have our prayer time the next night, I shared with Russ that I had remembered the times that God would call him to get up in the night. He shared with me the words that he spoke to God shortly before he broke his back. He proceeded to say, "Everyday Jo on my work truck, I knelt and prayed to the Lord. I told Him that I could hear Him calling me. I told Him not to break my back to get me to be obedient, that I was willing to do whatever He was calling me to do or to go wherever He wanted me to go." Obviously we realized when he had asked God not to break his back to get him to do God's will, that Russ was not meaning a physical break rather one of not having to hit him over the head to get him to move. The choice of words, "Don't break my back" ended up being a play on words.

We began to pray and asked God to be in control of our lives and the lives of our children through the difficult time we had begun to face. We specifically asked God to miraculously provide for our every need, which included the following: financial needs, wisdom and direction for myself to investigate the system for our financial needs, food, vehicle, peace for a colicky baby, patience for a strong willed child, but mostly for us to learn what God wanted us to learn in this time of suffering and for the restoration of Russ's back through surgery.

Life was not the same. I wondered if it would ever be. My thoughts wandered anywhere from being strong and courageous and encouraging to my husband's needs to some days behaving like the wicked step mother in Cinderella. When my husband would be in tremendous pain or even discouraged, I would touch him and pray for God's mercy and healing power. I would study in the Bible not just for my spiritual well being, but also to be able to give Russ scriptures that would comfort him. The scripture we clung to was Jeremiah 29:11,

"For I know the plans I have for you," declares the Lord, "Plans to prosper you and not to harm you, plans to give you a hope and a future..."

Another comforting scripture was Matthew 21:22,

"...if you believe, you will receive whatever you ask for in prayer."

I would tell Russ that he would not be in this kind of pain for the rest of his life. Surgery posed many fears. Russ was very anxious about having such major surgery. Again, I found myself saying to him, "God will not abandon you. He will pull you through. Only God can cause something good to come out of all of this. We're going to ask that it would be God's hands working through the hands of the surgeon." Russ had felt for quite some time that God had a call on his life. He strongly felt that he would be placed in a full time ministry doing the Lord's work. People think that this means becoming a minister. It does not necessarily. It could mean a minister, a youth pastor, a missionary, a musician, etc... Russ's gifts were in music, and in working with the teens. I would find myself praying, "Lord, I thank you for this place of suffering. Even though it is very difficult some days, I thank you that You are teaching us how to endure, persevere, and that You are building our character so that we will be stronger when we leave the valley and finally reach the mountaintop."

On December 2, 1998, my parents as well as my cousin Teri and my Aunt Karen came to visit our new baby and to pray for my husband and the surgery we faced in the morning. I remembered feeling so touched that they cared enough about our anxieties ahead of time *versus* just checking in after it was all said and done. It was at that moment that I realized there was no turning back. This surgery was going to happen, and the final outcome was in the Lord's hands.

In the meantime, I had to pray that my baby girl would take bottles for Nani since I had worked hard for a month prior to wean her from breast to bottle feeding. That night there was much to do, much to fear, and absolutely no sleep! There were bottles to prepare, and notes to leave for Nani and Grandma. I needed to make sure from a mommy's point of view that my boys had their favorite snacks and meals all ready and waiting for the sitters to fix. I wanted the day of daddy's surgery to be like any other day to them, and not one of fear and restlessness. So to me, if I could have my house in order for the children they would not feel the stress of our situation.

Russ and I had been trying to comfort one another as the uncertainties approached with every passing second. Would this surgery bring Russ relief from his pain and discomfort? Would he become paralyzed? Would he ever run and be himself again? My biggest fear of course was; would this be the last night that we could hold one another? We battled with our faith. One minute we were up, the next minute we were down. We both knew somewhere deep inside that our God was able. The two of us believed that God could instantly heal him yet we did not see that come to pass. Therefore we believed the answer and the only other choice was to proceed with the surgery. We also believed that God would see him through the surgery and that nothing would harm him. Yet there was an inner struggle to listen to our fears despite what our faith taught us.

Chapter Four

Waiting, Praying, Hoping For a Miracle...

December 3, 1998, greeted us with a crisp, chill in the air. Christmas was just twenty-two days away and everyone was feeling the buzz of the holiday. Santa was listening to bug eyed children as they sheepishly climbed upon his cushiony, red lap spilling out their last minute requests. Every commercial or television show was a constant reminder to all to begin your Christmas shopping if you had not already begun.

My children despite what our family faced with daddy's surgery; were still writing their Christmas lists, and continued flipping through the catalogs. I, on the other hand, was feeling more and more overwhelmed each and every day. Trying to wean a colicky baby from breast to bottle feeding was an enormous task. That bundle of joy at the time was a handful, and mommy was not finding much joy in being a new mother. There was the stress of a baby crying and demanding all of my time, a husband who was suffering in pain and needed constant care, and two boys to teach Monday through Friday, and music students to teach in the evenings. Our three year old was displaying every characteristic of a strong willed child, and my attitude began to border that of a manic depressant. I was up, and then I was down. Nothing could make me happy. Within a few months everything in my life changed. Most people have trouble with change. We become comfortable with the track we are on, and suddenly if our train jumps the track, we find ourselves faced with unimaginable fears. When our course has changed we find we have to switch gears in order to adjust to our new life.

The stress of the current changes began to mound. There were days I dreaded to climb out of bed. Finding time alone with God was something that I struggled with because my time was dispersed in so many different areas. I began to see over time that not making quiet time alone with the Lord in prayer and in reading the Word would be my downfall.

Russ and I showered, and brushed our teeth that December third like any other morning. His mother called from our driveway on her cell phone to tell us that she was there and to unlock the door because apparently we did not know she had been knocking. Russ of course was not allowed to eat or drink anything since the night before. My stomach was doing so many somersaults, that there was no way I could eat a thing. We made sure to sneak into the children's rooms to steal kisses and to say goodbye in our hearts so we did not wake them. Our hearts were already aching just thinking we would be separated from them because we did not know what the outcome of this surgery would be and how it would affect our family.

Russ's mother stayed with the children and my mother, father, and Russ's father went to the hospital with us. We traveled the familiar highways to the big city once again, and we hoped that once he recovered that we would be able to say goodbye to all the long trips to the doctor. Things moved so quickly once we were there and we remembered thinking, "Oh God, there is no turning back now!"

Russ was prepped for surgery, and the doctor and anesthesiologist met with us to explain what the surgery would involve, and what to expect afterward. I remembered getting all worked up and feeling uptight with those last few minutes wishing that all the months of lying in bed at night with him had not passed away so quickly, for I did not know if there would be any security there for me when this was all over. At least before surgery, even though he was in pain, he was still able to hold me at night and give me the security I needed through all of the changes that were taking place.

I prayed over him for God's divine protection, and for the surgery to be guided by God's hand. I prayed for God's mercy and speedy recovery, because Russ had suffered far too long, I wanted his nightmare, my nightmare to end. We sealed lips in our secret code for the last time, and they injected the medication that would send him to dreamland. I saw his eyes get heavy as we said goodbye.

"I love you Russ," I said.

"Love you," he replied.

Russ was out before they took him through the doors.

The waiting, the praying, the not knowing, was the hardest part. Suddenly I felt the tearing away from our four month old. Alexandra had depended on me to nurse her, yet was forced to be weaned because of the time I would have to spend apart from her at the hospital for days on end. This ate at me as I sat with my wheels spinning about the hell we had been living with the past year. Our parents tried to reassure me, and kept my mind set on God above. They prayed and paced as well. I could not imagine if I would have had to be alone that day in the hospital. I thanked God that they were there for us.

In an hour and a half the surgeon had come down to the waiting room looking for me. Mom and I had gone into the gift shop looking for cards of encouragement to give to Russ when his ordeal was over. My dad led the doctor to where I could be found. I remembered feeling like I was going to have to vomit. I felt that something had gone wrong, and before I knew it I suddenly felt as if this would turn out to be like some television movie where the doctor would inform the family of some dreadful news. The doctor had been preparing us for a three to four hour surgery. When your surgeon arrives in an hour and a half, naturally something does not seem right.

That was our doctor though, always overly optimistic. I'll never forget what my ears heard. "Mrs. Peters, it's over. He did GREAT! Everything went as planned; he's in recovery right now. Depending on how he's feeling he can go home tonight or in the morning."

"Can I see him?" I asked.

"Probably in an hour, he's pretty groggy. We'll be giving him morphine for the pain for a while. It's going to be important to get him up and moving as soon as possible. I'll be in to check on him tonight."

"Thank you, doctor."

"Hey, you take care now," he said.

Our parents and I went up to his room. When we approached his room we could hear him screaming and moaning in pain. In an instant, I saw the looks on our parents' faces and in their wisdom they knew something was not right and I reacted immediately. I charged into his room demanding to know what was going on. They were sitting him up and trying to put in a catheter because he had to go to the bathroom. Here he was just coming out of back surgery, and did not already have a catheter in place. How did they think he was going to get up and go to the bathroom within minutes of having surgery? I was outraged! To make matters worse, they were trying to put his back brace on over the area that had just been cut open. I came to the quick conclusion that this hospital did not know what they were doing!

I let Russ know that he was not alone with those whackos, and went back out in the hallway to inform our parents of what the commotion was all about. They too did not understand why a catheter had not been in place while he was in surgery. Everything started spinning out of control. I kept thinking, "An hour and a half for a three to four hour surgery, he can go home tonight or in the morning if he wants, and nurses putting in a catheter as well as putting a back brace on an incision minutes after having open back surgery." I started to feel like we had been taken. The craziness in my mind at that moment made me feel as if we were actors in some psycho movie where everyone was out to get us!

The hospital was overloaded, and short staffed, and was absolutely not displaying bedside manners at all. The next thing

I remembered was our parents saying that they were going to be leaving. I could not believe what I was hearing! I thought that in the movies at least, that family stayed what seemed like forever. Waiting, pacing, and taking turns visiting the patient. I remembered them asking if I was all right, or if I wanted a pop, but I felt I could not say, "What do you mean you are leaving me? I want, or need you to stay." I knew that my parents were trying to rush to my house to relieve Russ's mother from the children so that she could come to visit her son. Still in all, because of my emotional status, I still felt scared and abandoned.

Russ was doped up on morphine, and God knows what else at the time. He could not communicate, and was not in the best frame of mind when he came in and out of the medication's effects. Now I was truly alone and the sky grew dark as I stared out the hospital window. I watched the hustle and bustle of city life whirling around and the streetlights became one big blur as the tears began to fall. Everyone had lives of their own to live, and I felt like we had been thrown to the wolves. Where was our God, and why was this happening to us?

"Russ, can you hear me?"

"Uhh…I need more medicine," he stammered.

"I'll get the nurse, okay?"

There was no response, other than moaning from him. I was suddenly faced with having to muster up courage to make sure my husband was being taken care of properly. Everyone that loved or knew me, knew that I was soft spoken, naïve, and non-confrontational. I was the lion without the courage. I felt like I could take on the world with one hand tied behind my back, but would cower when the opportunity presented itself.

"Excuse me, my husband is in a lot of pain and is asking for some medicine. Is there something that you can give him?"

"Yes, mam. Someone will be right in."

About one-half hour later we were still waiting for the medicine man to arrive. It was up to the cowardly lion to brave the fronts.

"Excuse me, I'm sorry to keep bothering you, I know you are extremely busy, but someone was supposed to come and give my husband some pain medicine. It's been half an hour and no one has been in."

"Yes, mam. I'll get someone right on that. This is for Mr. Peters, right?"

"Yes, mam. Thank you very much."

"Russ...Russ..."

"Ughh...They coming with that?" he struggled.

I could tell between having been heavily medicated, and in tremendous pain, Russ was becoming very ornery. It began to stress me out even more, because I knew he must have really been in a lot of pain if he was getting angry about things. Russ was always easy going, easy to please, and easy to get along with. There would have to be quite a bit of havoc going on to rattle his cage.

"Mr. Peters, I hear you're in a lot of pain," shouted the male nurse.

Russ gave a garbled reply, "Yes!"

"This will help you, but I need to have you turn on your side a little bit. I need to give it to you in your leg, okay?"

I began to assist in rolling him since the nurse looked too frazzled to do it all by himself. Anytime Russ was touched to be moved, he would moan and groan in tremendous pain.

"AHH...ohh...gosh!"

I had never seen anyone poked and prodded so much in my life since this whole ordeal with his back began.

"It's okay honey, he's giving you a shot so you can relax and get out of the pain. It'll be all right," I said.

"That should help him be more comfortable now. He won't be able to have any more for a while though, just so you know," the nurse said.

"See, he's done. Do you want a sip of water?"

I had to talk to him like he was hard of hearing. I found that I was repeating myself several times because he was just too groggy from the medications to understand a thing.

"Water," he murmured.

I reached for his Styrofoam Cup of water, and held the straw to his lips.

"Okay Russ, sip."

He took little sips at a time. His mind was so cloudy from the drugs, and the pain confused him so, that he could not get his body to respond in the manner that he wished it would. Even drinking became something that he had to think about.

"Did you get enough, or do you want more?" I asked.

There was no response. He was out again, and there I was alone, over an hour away from home in a strange hospital with no one to turn to. I was in a lot of pain myself. My pain differed in the aspect that I did not feel strong for my husband or my family, and I was angry that no one was there to give us the strength we needed at that difficult moment in our lives. My heart broke more though to see the man I loved lying in a hospital bed, lifeless. A man stripped of all his strength, dignity, and faith. We were one, for better for worse, for richer, for poorer, in sickness, and in health. What hurt Russ pained me. I had become flesh of his flesh, bone of his bone when we united as husband and wife. He was not facing this tragedy alone.

"Lord, I pray that you touch Russ, and restore this broken back. He has been a faithful servant of yours. When you have asked him to go, he's gone. You've asked him to do this or that, he's always done it. Bless him now, for his obedience by lifting this pain. I pray that he will be able to get a good night's rest. Keep him from becoming discouraged oh Lord."

I began to become fearful of many things such as, finding the car in a dark garage, and finding my way home on busy expressways in the dark. I worried if the baby was taking bottles for my mother, and mostly about leaving Russ in that hospital when I would be almost two hours from him. I did not want to leave him, but I had three children waiting for me. That was a difficult part of our whole situation. I desperately needed someone to care for my broken heart and fears during this whole ordeal, yet everyone else needed me for something.

As I fought back the tears, I leaned over to kiss Russ and to inform him that I would have to leave. I knew that he did not want me to leave, so I told him that I would call and check in with the nurse's station to see how he was doing. I also talked up the next day and told him which one of the children I would bring with me. That was the first time we never kissed with our secret code. My heart ripped in two when I turned to walk out of his room.

The smell of the hospital made my stomach sour. I began to despise that I even knew this place because so much pain and fear was associated with it. I wanted so much to just go back to the way life was before all of this happened. So many memories flooded my mind that I began to get confused trying to find my way out of the hospital. Like a rat in a maze trying to find his way to the cheese, I wandered down corridors trying to get to the parking garage. Would I be at the right level? Would I be at the right end of the garage? What if someone begins to follow me, and there is no one around to help? Do I take a right or a left out of the parking lot? Which exit do I take first? What if something happens to Russ in the middle of the night, and I'm two hours away? What if I am asked to make some difficult medical decisions?

"God, help me," I prayed.

The Lord helped me to find my car safely, and the drive home in the dark was easier than I thought it would be. As I pulled into the driveway, I had more of a peace knowing I could unwind in the privacy of my own home and enjoy the children I had missed all day. I remembered walking into the house anxious to find out how well the baby did while I was at the hospital. I remembered my mother looking frazzled and tired. Immediately I nerved myself up feeling that I had expected too much from my mother that day. I worried that she was uptight that I had been gone so long.

"Hi, what's wrong with Alex?" I asked.

Alex was fussing up a storm, and my mother looked as if she did not know what to do with her anymore. My mother always had it together and nothing seemed to rattle her. I could tell she had just had enough. I remembered I wanted to cry. My emotions were raw and vulnerable, and I started seeing things that were not really there. My mother was not upset with me. She was tired, and she was probably a little frustrated because she could not settle the colicky baby down. Who wouldn't be? I always tended to read too much into every situation, that is who I am. Regardless, I was feeling pity for myself that my mother was not wooing over me, and concerned about all the fears that she did not know were racing through my mind. How would she know if I had not shared them with her? That was however, the state my mind was in that night.

When she left, I struggled to put the kids down for the night without daddy's help. The house seemed bigger, and scarier without Russ there to protect us. Every little noise concerned me. I climbed into bed and picked up the phone to call the hospital.

"Yes, this is Mrs. Peters. I was wondering if Russ is doing okay?"

"Hello. Yes, he's doing pretty well. He will be sore for a while ya know, but he just had some of his other medications so he should be set for the night. We don't foresee that there are any problems. He's going to the bathroom okay, and his incision looks good. He'll be fine; don't worry. The doctor will be in to see him tomorrow morning sometime, so if you have any more questions you can ask him then. Okay?"

"Thank you, and if you could, would you please tell him that I called and that I will be there in the morning?"

"Sure, you have a good night now Mrs. Peters."
"You too…bye."

My body, mind, and soul were spent. I had nothing left to give. If any of the children needed me in the night, I did not know if I could handle it. I wanted to cuddle the baby in bed to fill the void of her daddy being gone, but my body cried out for rest, and having a baby beside me would not have been the best idea. Memories began to flood my mind as I left the hospital that night. Before I knew it I was living many of them over as if I was actually there again. As I was lying awake remembering, I could still feel the surging hormones of that night when we began dating, and it made me miss him all the more. How I longed to kiss him, to be in his arms, and to have him tell me how he loved me again…

I learned real quickly not to believe everything even the doctors would say. Russ never made it home from the hospital the night of surgery, or the morning after. He stayed for five days. The doctor and nurses made him get up onto his feet immediately the day after surgery. Whenever he felt he needed to use the bathroom, or if they said that it was time for a stroll with the walker, someone would have to put him in his back brace, and help him to his feet. So far, everything that the doctor had told us from the beginning, I had reason to question. Nothing was as he had said. One medicine was not better than the next, Russ was no where near being able to return to work like he said he could, the surgery was completed much sooner than anticipated, and after it was all said and done, Russ took longer than stated by the surgeon to return back home. I could not help but feel we were everyone's guinea pigs, and that no one was looking after our best interests at all.

Each day that I had visited Russ in the hospital, I took one of the children, except the baby. Even though Russ was glad to see us, he was not in the mood to communicate. He was so ridden with pain that he just wanted to be left alone. Russ wanted our comfort, someone to sit and be close, but without the conversation. The kids had mixed emotions when they saw their dad. They missed him so, yet were devastated to see his state. Russ would repeat things several times not realizing it because of the heavy meds that he was on. I was frustrated more and more because I would have to repeat things, or constantly remind him of prior conversations. There were days that I felt as if I had another baby to care for.

The day arrived to be able to pick Russ up and bring him home. I arranged for his father to drive Aunt Kim's van so that we could lay Russ down in the back on an air mattress. We strategically planned the drive home purposely avoiding bumpy roads, sudden turns, and heavy traffic. His father was also our pastor and a great sense of comfort whenever we were in a struggle of some sort. After my father-in-law picked me up, we shared some scripture with one another, and prayed that we could get Russ home and comfortable. Russ's father told me that this time of difficulty would pass. He said, "I know this time has been very difficult, but God is going to see your whole family through. He is not far away from you guys, and He won't abandon you. You guys have been faithful servants to the Lord, and He has only the best in store for you." After my father-in-law had shared that with me, I had also remembered what the Bible said in Ecclesiastes 3.

"There is a time for everything, and a season for every activity under heaven..."

I shared with Russ's father that I had been studying in the book of Job. Job was a very righteous man and Satan went before the Lord several times and said that if Job were only tested with difficult situations, that he would surely curse God. The Lord proceeds to tell Satan that he could do anything that he wanted to Job but he was to spare his life. Through out the first few chapters, Job's family members die as well as his servants, livestock are stolen, his home was destroyed, and finally Job's health was struck. Job's wife became distraught to the point that she told Job to curse God and die. Overall, Job's wealth, livelihood, relationships, and health were ultimately tested. More so, was his relationship with the Lord. It says that Job never sinned against God in anything that he said or did while he was being tested. Job was pushed against the wall with no where to turn but to the Lord. I remembered thinking that Russ is being afflicted physically in much the same way, our financial situation was desperate, but we had a good family support system, a network of caring people at church, and a roof over our heads. Life was still good.

We arrived shortly after 11:00 A.M, and Russ was expected to eat his lunch before he left. I remembered walking into the room, and seeing a much more appreciative expression on Russ's face. He seemed a little more coherent than usual, and I believe he was more anxious to get home than we were to see him come home. He needed the comfort of things familiar, and to be allowed to be himself. If he wanted to scream in pain, I would let him. If he wanted to sleep all day, I would let him. If he wanted someone to get him things, or help him to do something, WE would do it. The hospital did a poor job of caring for their patients. Russ would have to wait a half an hour to an hour for a nurse to bring him in a bedpan. The old man in the bed next to him had an awful time when he needed assistance with his bedpan. The nurses would never come in on time. The man more often than not soiled himself. Pretty soon Russ and the old man would begin buzzing on behalf of one another, when the nurses would not respond to them personally. The old man would get so tired of hearing Russ moan in pain, that he would holler for someone to bring in his meds, to put him out of his misery.

I remembered the one day that I visited Russ; the nurses wanted him to take a stroll with his walker around the nurse's station, which would be quite a feat for someone who could not do anything by himself yet. I decided to keep him company while he walked. It was the slowest walk we had ever taken in our lives. To Russ it was progress since his previous trip around the station. I struggled so much more than him to see the improvements. Only Russ knew how he was feeling, in order to be able to judge whether or not there were any improvements at all, and I could only see the long road he had ahead of him and what that meant for me.

Russ ate his lunch and his father and I were starving, but we sat patiently waiting to get out of there. I had to dress him, and get his back brace on him in order for him to use the bathroom before we left. While he signed some paperwork and listened to the doctor's instructions, I packed everything as quickly as I could. I wanted to get my husband home where we could be ourselves, and try to settle into some kind of normalcy for the holiday. They brought a wheelchair, and we wheeled him away. All the madness we faced while we were there made us feel like we were being held prisoners. I could not help but feel like we had been being secretly used in some psycho movie the hospital was filming about how to cut them up, torture them, and leave them for dead. I wondered what would have happened if he had stayed just one more day.

We jostled Russ onto the air mattress in the back of the van. He hollered and moaned with every wiggle and tug to secure him into position. I sat on the floor up against the mattress to keep him from wiggling off. With the combination of Russ's dead weight on a squishy air mattress, the motion of the van would cause his body to move forward and backwards without moving the air mattress itself. It was a chore the whole ride home to keep Russ from being thrown forward, or out the back doors.

We started down the road, and Russ was in agony. He just wanted this whole ordeal to be over. He would keep mumbling, "Just hurry up and get me home!" His father's appetite got in the way before we hit the expressway, and before we knew it we were pulling into a McDonald's. I will never forget Russ's reaction. His father went to get out of the van to place his order, and Russ sarcastically hollered, "Get me a big mac will ya!" Russ was very irritable that day and perturbed that his father would take the time to grab something on the go while he was hurting and just wanted to get home. I was so embarrassed, and truly felt sorry for Russ treating his father in that way.

His father kept asking, "Do you want something? I'll get you something, what do you want?"

Russ just kept saying, "Nah…never mind…it's all right." The thing was; Russ was being cocky when he answered his father. I proceeded to tell Russ after his father got out of the van, that he was being uptight with his dad.

Russ said, "I am not!"

I said, "Russ, you're hurting, and the medicine is making you act differently. You might have hurt your dad's feelings. You better be careful with what you say."

By the time I had finished saying that to him, he would already have forgotten what he had said to his dad. It was so frustrating. What had happened to the man I had married? The man who had such wit, and never had a mean streak in his body? I felt as if I did not know him sometimes. I had to keep telling myself that it would be over soon and that things would be back to normal.

Chapter Five

The Monster Inside...

When Russ broke his back my life changed completely. Not only did I have a mother's role and a woman's responsibilities to handle, but all of a sudden I had to take charge of my husband's responsibilities that he could not perform any longer. There was stress beyond comprehension. We had a new mortgage to pay for, and a new life added to the family. I also schooled the children as well as taught music students to try to supplement our income while Russ was off of work. We were also very active in our church and because I was the Pastor's daughter-in-law, I felt I could not wear my heart out on my sleeve, yet remain strong for everyone else in the church body. It was very difficult to go to church and pretend to be happy because inside I was dying, and even though my husband knew what was going on, he did not know the severity of my mind's state. The last thing I felt like doing was helping others who were hurting. From that point on I began to battle with depression, but mostly anger.

The surgeon never prepared us that I would have to shower and bath my husband, dress him, get an orthopedic toilet for him, get him a walker, medicate him, change his dressings, and be emotionally stable for him. Obviously when I brought Russ home in that state and the baby cried to be fed or changed at the time I was showering him, I felt torn between the two people who needed me the most. My boys were forced to grow up quickly and learned to care for a baby while I took care of dad. Russ learned at times to be patient and understood that the baby sometimes just needed me and not her brothers. The boys had to learn to mow the lawn and shovel heavy snow so that I could be free to run a business to earn the money we needed. They had to drag heavy garbage out to the road even in the winter through three foot drifts. We pulled together and worked as a team, the kids and I. There was no one staying in the house for a day or two or on the weekend who could help with laundry, the baby, or fix supper for me, and I became very angry at the world that it all fell on me. There was also the legwork for our disability case, endless court hearings to prepare for, bills being sent to collection because worker's compensation was late in paying, days on end waiting for our checks to come and yet I still was expected to hold it together for five of us all at once.

When it would be time for follow ups, I would have to load up all the children for the day and drag them all along because there would be no one to watch them. When money was tight, I kept it to myself to manage the bills the best I could and tried to get assistance in any way, as if I had the time. There was absolutely no time for me. Every time I thought that I was in the clear of anyone needing from me, someone would get sick and demand more of my time, someone would have a nightmare, or my husband would take a turn for the worse and need to be taken to another doctor. I became selfish most of the time, and complained with every little task I had to perform. I did not enjoy the place where God had placed us and I wanted everyone to know about it.

When I would hear of anyone else in our families or our friends complain about not having money, or complain about their spouses or crisis, I felt like saying, "Shut Up! Do you not know how lucky you are that your husband can still work? Are you the one trying to get government assistance for your children? Would you rather have to bathe and feed your husband instead of having a little disagreement with him about something meaningless?" During this time of struggle for me, I began to realize that the resentment, unhappiness, and depression that I began to wrestle with were causing my mind and body to become sick.

Everything caused me to be angry, and I did not care about anyone else's needs or hurts, not even the man who I would seal lips with in our secret code. With each new day there would be new frustrations to deal with, and people's insensitivities and ignorance as to what we were really facing, or their hurtful words caused me to struggle with trusting and forgiving people. Unforgiveness turned into bitterness and resentment, which quickly turned into hatred. Because of the stress and this new rage and anger that were brewing gave permission in my eyes to be upset and angry about things that happened years before that did not matter anymore. For years I walked around with this hanging on me. No matter how many times I went before the Lord, this "thing" would not leave me. In the later years of dealing with anger and unforgiveness, I became oppressed by its hold. My body had many ailments, and I even began to flirt with the danger of eating disorders, punishing myself sick, not eating for long periods of time, and was over indulging with workouts for up to three or more hours a day. I was oppressed by this tormenting spirit that would have consumed me and led to what only God would know. Never in my life had there ever been anything as tormenting as this; it began to torture me day and night. My husband saw this evil and began to confront me, but I did not want to give him the satisfaction of telling me that there was something wrong with me. It was easier for years to have someone else to blame for my problems instead of trying to work it out and rid my body of the evil within. I was about to spin out of control, and no one would be there to pick me up, because no one else knew. My husband tried to be there for me, however, when he told me he understood what I was feeling, all I would be able to think about was how many times he had ever hurt me or disappointed me and my unbalanced way of thinking would cause me to become enraged, shut down, and withdraw from him and the family I was supposed to take care of. Therefore, I would not receive any advice from him. My mind and thoughts became grossly distorted. This is what my life became…

Out of Control...

"Why isn't anyone listening to me?" I screamed!

"What is your problem?" Russ asked.

"What is my problem? I'll tell you what my problem is. My problem is that I do everything around here. Jodi teaches the kids, Jodi teaches music students after she teaches the kids, Jodi does laundry, mops the floor, does the dishes, let's not forget, she fixes the meals, the bills, I do all the legwork for our disability case, take you to doctor appointments, and juggle many ministries at the church too! And nobody can find it within them to help me around here? No one cares about my needs! I need you to step in and help here, dear!"

"Hey, wait a minute. Whatever happened to just asking instead of getting all bent out of shape?" he asked firmly.

"Russ! Hello... that's part of the problem. Why should I have to ask? Why aren't you just stepping in and helping? I'm telling you I just can't take much more."

"Then maybe you shouldn't be teaching the kids, Jo. Maybe you can't handle it," he replied.

"Shut up! Do you see all the other mothers doing what I do, taking care of a husband that lives in chronic pain all the time? How can you say that I can't handle teaching the kids? It's not the teaching the kids that's the problem. Russ, why can't you understand how all of this is affecting me? It's not always about YOU!"

"You can do it yourself now! You don't treat me that way, and I'll tell you what, you better never talk to me like that in front of the kids again," he shouted.

"Russ, let me ask you something. When do my needs ever get met? Think about it. The answer is never! My spare time is spent fighting Social Security and Worker's Compensation in order for us to survive, calling and searching out new doctors and procedures in order to make a break through for your back, and let's not forget that I go to the appointments to fill out all the paperwork." No one ever says, "Let me take the kids for you so you and Russ can rest." Or, "Here's some supper, I knew you must not have felt like cooking after being at the hospital all day."

"Jo, I'm sorry. I know that since I broke my back everything's become twice as hard for you. You don't know how hard it is to see you doing all the things I can't do anymore. I am forcing this broken body of mine to go to college, trying to retrain for another vocation that I do not even know that I will be able to physically handle. I don't even know what to train for. If it's not pain I'm dealing with, it's my medicine making me into some person that I'm not! I will try to do more in order to take some of the load off of you, but I need you to keep in mind that going to school and sitting at home at the computer working on my college work increases my pain, you know that in the middle of the afternoon I can barely move. I don't even sleep anymore because I am constantly in pain. You make me feel like a jerk! I end up hurting before the end of the day, and you're already off the deep end. Then I feel that I can't ask you to rub my back, because I know that you'll get angry that there is just one more thing for you to have to do! I'm a thirty year old man who already feels like a burden to his wife; years before most people ever find themselves in this situation!"

"I'm sorry. I don't mean to make you feel like a jerk or make you feel that you are a bother to me. I'm sorry that you are always in so much pain, and that the doctors don't know what else to do for you! I am just reaching my breaking point. There are days when I am sick, and there is no one to fill in the gap for me. When I am at my breaking point, or I feel sick, I want so bad to lie down, or soak in a tub of hot water, but I don't get to. I can't go to the bathroom or take a shower in peace for crying out loud! People need from me all of the time, I need a break! When I am done teaching our kids at 2:30 in the afternoon, I teach music students until 7:00 P.M. Supper has to be fixed at lunch time so that when I am teaching it is all ready to be put on the table, and the housework is still being done up till 10:00 or 12:00 at night! When do I sit, when do I breathe, when is there time for me," I cried.

"Jo," he said as he hugged me tight. "I don't know what else to do. Maybe you need to drop some students. We really can't justify sending the kids into the school system. Let's pray and ask God to show us ways to change things around here." He wiped the tears from my face and suddenly I felt safe and had a sense of calmness about me, however, in the back of my mind I knew things would not change, because as long as he had this disability, my life would never be the same. We were one, what affected him, affected me, and my reactions would affect the others. The devil was destroying my hope of ever having a normal functioning family, he was robbing me of the joy of my salvation, and he was killing me with a seed of unforgiveness. Depression lurked in the shadows of my mind. I was right, it did not end here.

I remembered a specific instance that happened right before I placed myself into counseling. This was the eye opener for me. This was also the first time I fully saw this monster that had been growing inside of me for years! When I saw it emerge, I was horrified. The stench of hell could be smelled in the room, and an eerie chill went right to the core of my being. How could a child of God have this monster oppressing them? What happened to me that allowed this thing to grow? Most importantly, I asked God, "What am I supposed to learn from this?"

My husband and I had just returned home from a weekend with our youth group just hours before this given incident. Our teen retreats took approximately seven months of planning and hard work. We have to say goodbye to our own children for the weekend which is always difficult to do. When we return home from one of these retreats, our minds, bodies, and souls are completely spent and exhausted! Because of my need to protect those close to me I can not reveal the depth of my struggles or at times how ugly things in our home actually became, so I will only touch the surface to give you an idea of how much worse things did get from here. Choosing not to forgive people has a way of damaging events or relationships that absolutely have had nothing to do with your situation that caused you great pain to begin with. It distorts your psyche, and effects your mood overall.

A situation arose in our house when I was not in a right state of mind. I was very enraged, and I had been irritable all week. I had been slamming doors, cupboards, and barking orders to the kids day after day. I suppose that anyone's spouse would have had enough. That night my husband had. At that point I do not even remember what had happened to our kids. I think the baby had already been put to bed and I imagine that my two boys heard the fighting and went to their rooms or fell asleep in front of the game. The next thing I knew, I slammed shut our bedroom door, locked it, and barricaded it with my own body. This was going to be the last time I dealt with this, even if it meant that one of us was going to get hurt! His nostrils were flaring like a bull ready to charge the red flag. He had taken enough of my roller coaster mood swings, insults, and abuse that he could not stomach even being around me anymore. I was going to have things out, because I was so tired of holding everything together for everyone else, and everyone needing from me, and burying unresolved issues inside which was the result of me always feeling the way I did. It always came down to, I was right and he was wrong.

As my body barricaded the door, I hurled more insults. I was furious! My blood was past the boiling point this time, and I had a feeling that this fight would determine something in our relationship. He began demanding that I remove myself from the door so he could leave. His experiences with my rages told him either way he was doomed, besides the fact that he did not want to hurt me physically or verbally. He was trying to do the right thing by removing himself calmly until things had cooled down enough to where we could talk and think clearly. My stubbornness however, was not going to allow him to escape my damnation this time.

"Open the door, Jo!"

"No, I'm not opening this door until we get to the end of this!" "I am not staying in here, and I am not sleeping in here tonight either, so move it," he screamed. He approached me and tried to get a grip on the door, but I pushed into him in order to keep him from leaving the room. He became more irate at this point and said, "Get out of my way!" Of course the night was filled with profanities, we entered into uncharted waters; would our relationship ever be the same?

I knew I had pushed the envelope this time, yet felt justified in my actions. Russ had never hurt me physically, mentally, emotionally, or verbally. I was the monster that had pushed this innocent man in the corner of the boxing ring. It was as if the whole time he spent in the ring he had been bound and gagged.

Now that I look back upon this, it reminds me of the scripture in Isaiah 53:7,

"He was oppressed and afflicted, yet he did not open his mouth; he was led like a lamb to the slaughter, and as a sheep before her shearers is silent, so he did not open his mouth."

Russ's behavior symbolized that of Jesus's because insult after insult, accusation after accusation, He pretty much kept silent. This time he snapped! He knew in my state of mind that nothing he could say or do would change anything. He knew I had a problem and that I needed help. It was like trying to help an alcoholic or a drug addict, who could not see the error of his or her ways. They remain unwilling to change. Therefore, there was nothing that Russ was going to be able to do. I was not even sure if he loved me anymore since he had called me that name. I saw something change in him at that same moment, and the fear and reality of what I had started sank in. "What if I never get that part of him back? What if I damaged things beyond repair? Is my God able to deliver us from this evil?"

Things remained heated in our bedroom. I wanted to hurt someone else so bad because I was tired of suffering alone with no one understanding my pain. When you hurt so bad for so long, you want others to feel your pain and be miserable with you. Russ however, saw the hook, line, and sinker, and would not bite. "No, you are not leaving this room, I want answers," I said. "You're stupid, you know that! I hate you!" At that point Russ picked up his pillows and blanket and was determined to exit the room since my tantrum had led me away from the door. When I saw him headed for the door I shoved him very hard, and pounded on him over and over. When I saw his back give and his legs buckle underneath him, I instantly saw the Monster! The scales fell off of my eyes, and I could see everything for what it was! My husband was not a wimp allowing himself to be womped on by a woman! I was the one out of control; he only loved me through it and prayed for the Lord to intervene. I could not even pray for myself let alone him.

My husband was himself enduring a very difficult time with a disability with his back that left him unable to do sometimes even the simple things that we take for granted. Russ could no longer mow his lawn, take out heavy garbage, carry his heavy music equipment, drive for long distances, run, play sports with his kids, or even wrestle around with them. He no longer worked a regular job, but instead was going to college and was hopeful to someday become employable once again. Some of the simple things in which he had to change to cater to his back for instance were the way he brushed his teeth, shaved, and tied his shoes. Bending over, or leaning forward for any reason was no longer something that he could do. These are just a few of many areas that had greatly changed in the man's life. I had neglected to see what he was struggling with all this time, and made the whole focus to be on me!

This was the man I loved. This was the Knight in Shining Armor that had swept me off of my feet, who stole a kiss in our secret code whenever he could, a righteous man full of integrity despite what he could not do in his flesh anymore. A light went on in that dark moment, and instantly I saw that Russ was still all of those things and more, however, our relationship could not help but be changed after all we had begun to face. Love and relationships would have to be worked at now; held more precious, and cherished each day as if we were in our last moments.

I saw embarrassment in his eyes, and humiliation that I, his beloved spouse, who was supposed to protect and understand his feelings of his disability, destroyed in a matter of seconds. When I had shoved him against the dresser that night and saw his back and legs buckle, I knew I had ruined him for a moment in time and I was sick at heart that I had failed him and let him down. He would never be able to trust me again, or so I thought. I took the most painful, and humiliating thing that could happen to a man and exploited it even though it was only the two of us in the room that night. A part of him had always tried to hold onto some type of dignity when he became disabled, because he was supposed to be my protector, my provider, my "Knight in Shining Armor." Since the day of his injury, he has had great trouble in trying to feel like he fit any of these requirements anymore. By me exposing his "nakedness" by stripping away any decency he had left, I had totally ruined him, and I could not take it back. What I had done was worst than the evil I had been wrestling with for years. I started crying, "I'm so sorry, please don't go…I just want you to hold me…please let's start over… please just hold me!" "Lady, get out of my face!" "Please Russ,

I need you, I'm sorry!" "No, I'm not touching you now, move out of my way!" There was nothing more that I was able to do. I had to let him go. He had controlled himself by not hitting me when he probably really wanted too, and the thing is, I knew he was right, and that I was wrong, just like all of the other times. I just did not understand why I always felt so strongly that he was so deserving of my abuse when deep down inside I knew he was right about everything.

The cycle always repeated itself. After every fight I found myself over the toilet, banging my head against the wall, or ripping at my skin trying to hurt somewhere else other than my heart. We went two weeks without speaking or touching one another. That is when I decided to go for help. It would be a year and a half before I would receive my deliverance! My doctor voiced his concern about my schedule of home schooling, running a business out of my home, activities at church, a new baby, and a husband living in chronic pain. He suggested that I make changes in my life to reduce the stress level. I told him I had thought about going to counseling, just to unload and then maybe I would be able to see the whole picture through someone else who was on the outside looking in.

Although counseling was a step in the right direction, it did not bring the complete deliverance that I needed. More than a year continued with things quite calm in comparison to the night of *hell* in our bedroom. I could see that the devil was causing destruction, and that he was trying to destroy the work and the ministry that God had for us. Over the course of that year's time, I had begun to confide in my mother and I do not know what possessed me to do so. Finally, the "Monster" started to rear its ugly head about a year and a half after our last episode. To avoid another confrontation of many regrets, I called my mother and told her that I would be coming down that night to spend the night. I needed to have absence make my heart grow fonder for my husband.

What I failed to mention earlier was the fact that our family since my husband's disability had been together 24/7. We were never apart. We were constantly getting on one another's nerves. My husband and I needed time apart. I told my children that I was going to go stay the night with one of my girlfriends. I informed them that I might not be coming home until the next night, so they would not worry. I had responsibilities at home so therefore, I only had a few hours to go away, and I knew they would fly by, and yet there would be moments that would seem like an eternity.

I waited for my children to go downstairs to play so that they would not see me leaving with a suitcase. I did not want to scare their little hearts. At this point I was clearly unsure if this excursion would turn into more than a day or so. Every time that I was ready to leave, my mother would call and say that it was storming, not to come out yet. It would be fine where I was. It would then storm at my house and be fine at my mother's. This continued for an hour or so. I finally chanced it, the whole time holding secret conversations with my mother so my husband would have no idea where I would be.

"Bye. Enjoy your time of peace while I am gone," I said.

It was the hardest thing that I had to do. Russ and I never parted without saying, "Love You!" Usually if we had been arguing, we still locked our lips in our "secret code" and made amends.

I had arrived at my mother and father's house. It was dark and I felt hollow not having my little family with me. My father, I do not think, had any idea of what was going on, or at least he did not know the details of our situation. I will never forget the look I saw him caste at my suitcase when he walked by the room. The Olympics were on, and we were going to have a good time watching our favorite competitions. I tried to harden my heart, so I would not break. I did not want to talk about my problem, or my heartache. I tried to make believe that all I wanted to do was to have a sleep over with mom and dad and watch the Olympics. My mother was wise to that however, and late that night right before bed, she asked, "How are things going?"

I began to pour out the intimate details of how bad this tormenting spirit had been for years, and how I did not know how much I loved Russ any more. It was funny, I was saying how I did not know how much I loved him, yet found myself defending him every chance I had. I knew he was right, I knew he was innocent of any of my accusations, insults, and abuse. I knew I did not love him like God told us to love. It was me, me, me! I just wanted my daddy to make it all better. I wanted to curl up and die; I truly did not want to go on anymore. My mother continued to tell me that the devil was trying to destroy us, and God's plan, and that somewhere down the road I had listened to his lies for so long that eventually he began to torment me over and over again. What I did not share even with my mother at that point was that I struggled with punishing myself. Whenever anyone especially my husband would show any disapproval in their voice, I would feel like a fat, ugly, slob and hate myself.

My mother came and sat next to me on the couch and began to pray, and that's when I lost it. I began to sob like I was in my daddy's arms again; a helpless little girl who had lost her way, thinking that she had everything that she ever wanted to make her happy, but bought the lie of the devil and was hanging on the edge of losing it all. My mother was scared for me; I could see it in her eyes. I had always seemed to be on top of any problem and knew that God would have his way in every situation. This time however, she saw hollow eyes, desolation, and a mangled tormented mind that was screaming FREEDOM! Her praying became more pressing. She became angry at the devil for lying to her little girl, for consuming her every thought, and for trying to steal her away. She commanded Satan to leave me alone. She spoke to him to release the grip he had on me. I have to laugh when I have to speak somewhere and retell the story of my mom's prayer of deliverance for me. I explain that she practically sat on top of me shoving my head down into the cushions of the couch rebuking the devil!

That prayer of deliverance set me free that night. I walk, live, and think as a different being. I no longer have nightmares, or have tormenting spirits that lie to me. Satan tried that next night to throw things at me. I cannot say that the opportunities have not been there for me to walk back into my old life, because there are opportunities everyday, however, I choose to walk in deliverance, to thank God everyday my feet hit the floor that I am not bound by that spirit. I speak to the devil and tell him that I am not bound, and that my mind has been renewed in the name of Christ. Romans 12:2 states,

"Do not conform any longer to the pattern of this world, but be transformed by the renewing of your mind. Then you will be able to test and approve what God's will is—His good, pleasing and perfect will."

That is the measure in which I stand on every day. Since I've taken steps in doing just that, I began to see much clearer that our situation was just beginning to fulfill the plan God had for our little family. By renewing my mind in Christ, there are a few simple things that I have applied to my life. They are the following: guard your mind, your thoughts, and spend time in the Word and in prayer daily.

God tells us in 2 Corinthians 10:5,

"We demolish arguments and every pretension that sets itself up against the knowledge of God, and we take captive every thought to make it obedient to Christ."

Since my deliverance God's opened my eyes and shown me things to be aware of that would have great potential to cause me once again to struggle with unforgiveness. Be careful who you let close to you. Guarding your heart and mind sometimes means to be choosy about your company, for some it enters into family relationships which makes it tough, because most people cannot or will not part with family. If someone likes to talk and cause dissention God warns us to stay away from them. Whether it is friend or family, acquaintance or co-worker, if someone is betraying you and painting an ugly picture of you to anyone they can, then put an end to anything beyond being cordial. If their tongues like to wag about you and your affairs, if they try to cause problems between you and your spouse or children, do not have anything to do with them. Contempt breeds contempt, hate breeds hate, and therefore the cycle will continue.

"A perverse man stirs up dissension, and a gossip separates close friends," Proverbs 16:28.

"There are six things the Lord hates, seven that are detestable to him: haughty eyes, a lying tongue, hands that shed innocent blood, and a heart that devises wicked schemes, feet that are quick to rush into evil, a false witness who pours out lies, and a man who stirs up dissension among brothers," Proverbs 6:16-19.

If someone is stirring up trouble and discord among those God has called for ministry, then God does not look fondly upon it, and justice will be avenged.

Proverbs 6:12-15, *"A scoundrel and villain, who goes about with a corrupt mouth, who winks with his eye, signals with his feet and motions with his heart---he always stirs up dissension. Therefore disaster will overtake him in an instant; he will suddenly be destroyed without remedy."*

Surround yourself with those whose feet are planted in the rock, those who do not waiver in their faith, and those who are not tossed by the waves of life's storms.

When an unclean thought or a lie from the devil is thrown at you, recognize where it is coming from, and command it to flee from you in the name of Jesus and it will. Speak out of your mouth every day that you have been set free from the bondage that you were delivered from. Refuse to walk the old path of bondage, so that nothing will cause you to turn back to your vomit. Lastly, become intimate with Jesus, daily feeding upon His Word; spend time in prayer and share with others how He has delivered you from your struggles.

The Bible says, *"They overcame by the Blood of the Lamb and by the word of their testimony."* (Revelation 12:11)

Chapter Six

No More Monsters Just Darkness...

At the time I had put myself into Christian counseling I did so in order that I could see our situation from a different perspective, through someone else's eyes hoping that I could find a better balance to all of my responsibilities, be stronger for everyone that needed me, but mostly for healing inside. As I was on the road to recovery and was able to manage my responsibilities with the help of an anti-depressant, the Lord opened my eyes to other things that began to turn up out of nowhere to try to cause me more pain and grief. We pinpointed that with me being on the road to recovery the devil was going to come in the back door, and use people's hurtful words to wound me and cause me to harbor unforgiveness again. By coming in the back door, you see, it would not be as recognizable to me. However; when people who are close to you lie, or do things to purposely hurt you the truth is, it is hard to forgive. So for the next year or two that is what the devil thought he could do to me, but instead, after prayer, and taking time to cool down, my husband and I felt that it was best to deal with these issues by confronting these people.

There were obvious situations that arose where people's words were meant to destroy us and our marriage. The first wound was finding out that there were lies circulating as to the real reason I was in counseling. Information about our private sufferings had also been shared with some people outside of the family which bothered us because when you are in a place of suffering there are just some things you do not want the whole world knowing. Personal pain is a very private matter and needs to be respected. The Lord showed me right then and there that dissention was brewing and that it was not of Him. I knew the truth, and the truth would set me free! What were these people trying to gain at my expense?

The second thing to happen came from a woman we had known for years, but her words were so destructive and damaging and absolutely should have never been said to me. It dealt with our past and was said purposely to hurt me. The thing that made it a double blow was that my children were within ear shot of hearing it. I could not get over what I was hearing. What I kept asking myself was, what does what you just said lady have anything to do with me, my children, my husband and the pain we are enduring? Here our family was suffering in more ways than one and now I have a grown woman saying horrible, insulting things to me. I had more important things to focus on, and no time to mess with people's insults and their own jealousies and insecurities.

The third very painful thing said to us was in regards to being on disability. There were surprisingly many people who were very nosey, inconsiderate, interrogating, and down right rude. My mind and spirit immediately recognized where these horrible accusations were coming from. It made me feel that everyone including family, friends, neighbors, and Channel 7 news (not really, but might as well have) had us under microscope watching our every move and every dollar spent because we were on disability. I immediately became very leery of who I talked to or who I trusted. We did not know who would turn on us next. I could instantly feel in my mind the struggle coming again. Eating at me day and night were thoughts of, "What were our family and friends let alone neighbors and acquaintances really saying and thinking of us?"

There would prove to be many other words to cut like a knife. Then I realized if I let myself get wounded over every little oversight, or insult, I might as well dig a hole and bury myself alive, because the more you dwell on things said or done out of spite or ignorance, you'll be buried alive in pain and unforgiveness. I lived that once and refused to ever live it again. I decided that if people could be cruel and so blunt as to say inconsiderate things, especially with my children in earshot of it, then I could be blunt not cruel back. We take things to prayer, and sometimes now we confront these issues and expose things to the light, and ask people why they do these things.

Russ and I have come to the realization that whoever it is that we are cordial but we have no desire to spend quality time with these people especially when they offer no forgiveness for what they have done and you know they have not changed. My mother always said, "God doesn't expect you to be a doormat." We forgive as Christians do, but we can't forget, and no one in their right mind wants to be burned again. I had been through too much and decided for my health and the sake of my family's well being that I was not going to be manipulated by anyone again and if they were offended then they would go prey on someone else.

So even despite the monster leaving me, the darkness of my husband's disability still lingered. Seven years after it all began, we found ourselves in pretty much the same place with his back, and the effects of all the drugs, and later the withdrawals complicated our lives more. I had no more struggles trying to maintain my sanity because I had taken the necessary steps to reduce the stress for all of us by placing the children in the public school system instead of home schooling. I scaled back on how many music students I would teach, even though it meant sacrificing some money. I started to wise up and say no to people who asked for this or wanted me to do that.

Russ was a little further ahead in his college studies, but still had a ways to go, and I decided in the spring after everyone else was settled into a school routine and all was well, that I would go back to college myself. My reason was to receive an education in case my husband could not finish college or become employable again. However; I found myself pregnant with our fourth child at the end of my first semester. Russ was getting ready to face trying the spinal cord stimulator which is a unit placed along the spine that sends electrical stimulation to the parts of the body where chronic pain exists. Instead of the body feeling pain, it feels a numbing or tingling sensation instead. In a couple of months we would have our first consultation with yet another surgeon this time at Buffalo General.

The doctor explained exactly what was involved, the statistics of failure rates and success rates as well as the risks involved. At this point this was the only thing left to try. For seven years we had traveled to pain treatment clinics for doctors to say that Russ was out of their league. I even had traveled out of state to Mayo clinics for the best of the best. Every medicine, procedure or new doctor left us disappointed and without any answers. Russ had been poked and prodded and should have been placed in the Guinness Book of World Records for being the world's biggest guinea pig! Many nights were spent searching the web for some new break through. We also endured seeing and hearing of others receiving healings or recovering from their back surgery with record speeds and could not help but feel at times that God had abandoned us.

Quickly I would be reminded of the Footprints in the Sand story. The truth was that God had not moved, yet was still carrying us. The spinal stimulator would have to be done in a trial phase first to prove whether or not a permanent one would be beneficial. So in May of 2005, two months after we discovered I was pregnant again, we went in for the trial. Two leads of about eleven inches were placed along the spine and an outside battery pack was temporarily attached for him to experiment around with. The battery pack was hooked up to the wires that were implanted, Russ could then turn the stimulation up or down according to the relief that was needed. There were specific things that the doctor would be looking for to be able to tell if the trial had been a success or not. The first would be whether or not stimulation was giving a substantial amount of relief.

Secondly, would Russ's physical activity increase without the pain increasing? Thirdly, would he gain more hours of sleep a night, and fourthly, would he use less pain medication? After two nights in the hospital the doctor was ready to call it quits and take everything out because Russ was still trying to recover from the procedure that none of the benefits of the trial were evident to any of us. We were extremely disappointed, because we hoped this was finally the answer we had been waiting for. Now with the stimulator implant and a new baby coming, we thought it must surely be the perfect ending to all of this. The doctor wanted to give the trial one more day. He told us if Russ did not sleep any better that night that he would not do the permanent one. Our whole church and more prayed like never before.

The phone rang at 6:00 A.M. the next morning, it was Russ and he informed me that he had slept for seven hours straight, which is something he had not done for seven years. The permanent stimulator would be scheduled in a week's time! We were elated and I honestly felt that everything was finally over. They unhooked the battery pack but left the leads sewn in along the spine, for they would be the wires used for the permanent stimulator. We went home and were told to expect his pain to worsen which is the back side of the trial phase. If it was working in the hospital, and then he goes home a week without it, we will then realize how much it had really been helping after all. These were all things to take into consideration. His pain was worse than usual and it seemed a lifetime away before he would have the permanent one in place. All in all, the kind of results we had hoped and prayed for. The permanent one was implanted and Russ said on a scale of 1-10 with 10 being the worst pain that his legs usually averaged an 8 or 9, with the stimulator, they were now a 1. A dramatic improvement! His back usually averaged an 8 or 9 and was now around a 4. We felt there was significant improvement and were excited about Russ moving on with his life after the six week recovery period was through.

Once through recovery he started noticing that his back was not getting the relief he had once felt. His legs however, were still good. According to the doctor, patients who tend to have the low back pain like Russ, tend to get great relief to the extremities however, the back is not helped that much. The reason for this is because of the narrowing of the area of the spine where the pain is located. It does not allow enough of the electrical current to pass through. The adventure then became getting off of his medicines that he had been on for seven years. Narcotics, anti-inflammatory drugs, muscle relaxers and stomach coaters. The withdrawal symptoms were worse than the disease is what I had always heard, and I almost had to agree with it, except for the medicine did help him immensely. Both of us did not see how he would ever live without it even with the implant. When Russ was at his worst, he would be taking sixteen to eighteen different pills a day for pain and inflammation. Four months outside of having the implant, he had lowered his medications to only three or four pills a day and is in the process of becoming totally drug free. The medicines really played a huge role in our communication. There were days Russ would call me from town and ask where he was supposed to be! I couldn't rely on him for bank transactions, important calendar dates, and important phone messages. There were many arguments and upheavals in our lives because of it. The fact was the medicine had changed him. As he began to come off of the oxycontin he became very agitated, short fused and very sick. As far as the implant was concerned and according to doctors it would be a waiting game because for some patients they are helped for the first five years and then received no benefit thereafter. Everything needed to be and was in God's control, we had to let go, and that was hard.

The permanent battery pack had to be implanted at the top part of the buttock. This along with the scars of surgery on his back was something my husband was concerned about, but I loved him and always would. To me, I just wanted my husband whole again. I wanted to do whatever it took to get this man that I loved whatever it was going to take to make him the old Russ I had married and started a family with. Once again as Russ recovered from this implant, I would have to help him shower and dress, as I did with the first surgery he had seven years ago, this time pregnant again! I never minded, but to Russ it was his pride on the line.

    I must say that I am proud of how strong he has been through all of this. He never seemed to battle with the depression like I did, although there were three or four times he was real discouraged. I know I would not have been able to endure the length of his illness had I been the one dealing with chronic pain. I had been so depressed and at one point close to a break down, that I could not get out of bed in the morning, let alone take care of the house and family. One thing Russ always struggled with was the fact that he could not provide anymore, and hated with a passion that things were always so tight financially and that I had to do more than the average wife because of it all. Another thing was that there were so many things that needed to be done around the house, and physically he had great difficulty trying to keep our house and vehicles maintained. Our family was great. Many times they sacrificed their time to help fix things, gave us money to get them fixed, babysat or even went to appointments with us. Without our family and church family, how would we have survived? Everyone's prayers carried us through it all. Up to this very moment we do not have anymore answers for his back, or places to turn. Our backs, no pun intended, are up against the wall. The Lord is where we lay our trust, hopes, fears, and dreams.

    We know that, *"We can do all things through Christ Jesus who strengthens us."* (Phillipians 4:13)

Because of our faithfulness in tithing through all of this, we see this as the only reason why we have been sustained and not loss our house, our cars, or even our marriage. God has provided so many times that we have never been without. Even when the figures in our budget did not add up, there was somehow always enough to pay our bills, and get what we needed. We know and believe that God can still do a miracle in his back even with the stimulator in place. We now look at life differently, prioritize the things in our life differently, and hold life and the things taken for granted more precious. What will be our focus is to answer the call of God we have felt on our life, and strive to fulfill what He has for us. If we are called to pastor, we will pastor. If we are called to move, we will move. If Russ will never be able to carry his music equipment again, then someone else will. We will not move from the will of God. We will listen, follow and take up our cross each day. God will make whatever the call is on our life alright with our souls.

Our children's faith has grown as well. They have not gone unaffected by all of this. Since all of this began our children are now sixteen, eleven, seven, and baby Collin. Devon and Brennan remember when their dad used to wrestle, hike, and never be in pain. They saw him change, and watched their mother have to care for their father, and even had to learn heavy responsibilities at early ages because daddy could not do it anymore. Alexandra and Collin will never have known him any other way but with this back problem. This to them is normal. Alex still does not fully understand other kid's dads working. We have told her about daddy's job and that is how he was hurt, but that was never a part of her life, so she does not fully comprehend it. We have to believe there is a purpose under heaven for all of what has happened from the painful words to marital struggles, to disabilities, to day to day life situations, all of these are lessons to be learned from.

I like to think that one of the purposes is to write this book for others who face life changes that are overwhelming, and feel whether Christian or not, that they can't go on anymore. I have survived and become stronger as a whole. I even managed to come off of an anti-depressant and carry on very well without the help of medicine. It is never too late for counseling, for a closer walk with God, for healing, or especially for forgiveness. Some of these will be worked on for a life time. Others are temporal. However; no matter what,

"Jesus is the same yesterday, today, and forever."
(Hebrews 13:8)

PART TWO
Φ

Using your tools

Chapter Seven

A Gerbil In a Spinning Wheel...

We all have certain things in our lives that we have a hard time lying down. How many times in your life have you found yourself hung up on the same problem time and time again? You may feel you have truly laid your burden down at God's feet and somehow, somewhere down the road you have picked it up again. Why in the world do we do something as stupid as that? Why, when God tells us to lay it at His feet, do we feel later on that He needs help in handling our problem? How come it is so difficult to just steer away from it when we see it on the side of the road? Part of the answer to that question is simply that we are human beings with carnal minds. It is very difficult to think and to always have the mindset of God. God is perfect; He lacks in nothing. We however, fall short of the mark every time. We want to have control over every aspect of our lives. In a strange way, this is a defense mechanism for driving away any possibilities of discomfort, pain, or inconvenience that may be thrown in our way. When we meddle and get in the way of God's process of picking up our burden so that He can carry us through, we typically make it harder on ourselves, thus we take twice as long to get through our circumstance.

By continuing to pick up that problem over and over, we are like gerbils on a spinning wheel going 'round, running faster and faster to get away from the problem that causes us great pain and or requires so much endurance that we spin the wheel out of control or fall so hard and fast that we collapse and get tossed off only making us more determined to repeat the process again once we get our second wind. If we were to sit and observe a gerbil doing the same thing we actually do in our own lives, we would laugh and see how ridiculously this creature was behaving. Why do we not see it in ourselves?

It requires great faith to lie something that seems so large and unsolvable at the feet of someone who we have never seen. Even if we have heard His voice before, even if we have talked and walked with Him for years, we have never beheld the face of God. It seems impossible to know that He is who He says He is and that He will do what He says He will do. It is hard enough to believe and to have faith in the people we love at times, let alone to have faith in a god we have never touched or seen. To have faith is to believe in things we cannot see. If we only have faith, the Lord will show us things that we will be able to keep in our hearts; things that in the long run will help us to be strong and will help us to avoid picking up our baggage again. Attaining such faith is a journey, a journey that will not be an easy one, a journey that may take a lifetime to perfect.

What other choice do we have? There is nothing else to turn to. Anything the world has to offer may provide a thrill or a high for a season, but when the thrill is gone, you are left with only addictions, or depression. You find yourself on another spinning wheel, which completely keeps you from the only One who can set you free. If we are kept from the One who can set us free, then we are on the wrong road, headed for destruction. There is nothing sadder than someone who has walked hand in hand with the Father, and then turns away.

"No one who puts his hand to the plow and looks back is fit for service in the kingdom of God." (Luke 9:62)

"All have turned away, they have together become worthless." (Romans 3:12)

How can God use us if we turn away, especially when life is difficult? Those that do turn away from Him completely will always be miserable, for they have tasted of the vine but have chosen to spit it out. After that anything else that is tasted will be bitter by comparison. As a great friend of mine says, "There is no greater life and we're living it!" This does not mean this great life will be a rose garden, or that we will not come across a thorn or two. No matter what, walking with the Father is a great life. We are never alone.

We have used the comparison of spinning wheels to picking up the baggage we thought we had laid down for the Lord to carry. What was not pointed out was the fact that a gerbil lives in a cage as well. He is not completely free even though he has room to run. As long as we keep ourselves in a cage and do not trust God to open the door, then we cannot run from that spinning wheel that seems to attract us time and time again. Getting hung up on that wheel will make us tired and weary. It takes more strength to run 'round and 'round than it does to bend over and lay something down. When will we see the real picture? Ask the Lord first to help you lay down that burden. Secondly, ask Him to help you move far away from the spinning wheel. Thirdly, ask Him to open the cage door. There is an overwhelming feeling of freedom when we can pull ourselves away from that spinning wheel.

Chapter Eight

Being a Tool and Using Your Tools...

It is amazing how being used as a tool for the Lord in places of ministry can actually teach us as well as the ones the Lord has placed in our care. Many times we will find that when we are in the midst of a battle of some sort that words, scriptures, or songs God calls us to use in our ministry end up ministering to ourselves more than to those around us. How wonderful that something we think God is intending for us to use as words of teaching, healing, or encouragement for those in our care, tend to bring healing and remembrance of scriptures to help us cope with what we face.

Sometimes we feel that just because we are placed in a ministry, we cannot have any problems in our lives. We feel ashamed or embarrassed to admit to anyone, even our spouses, or those who are the closest to us that we are falling short of the mark and are not as perfect as people think we should be. As Christians we need to minister not just to the unsaved, but also to one another.

"If one part suffers, every part suffers with it; if one part is honored, every part rejoices with it." (1 Corinthians 12:26)

Many of us who are very active in the church, and tend to hold down more than one ministry at a time, seem to have few opportunities to be on the receiving end of the ministry in our time of need. While always trying to be strong for everyone else, we begin to deceive ourselves into thinking that we are invincible. In order to prevent burnout people in places of ministry need to be very cautious as to how much they take on. They need to spend more quiet time with the Lord, reading and studying the Word, and praying than does the average Christian.

We are tools in the Master's hand. He picks us up and uses us where we will best be used. Sometimes it is not where we wish to be, and we cannot understand what in the world is going on. We've all asked this question, "I'm not sure this is where I should be God. Why are you planting me here?" Regardless, our job as a tool in the Master's hand is to just do the job required. He considers our characteristics, personalities, and circumstances that make up who we are.

God gives us five basic tools to use to help us cope with life's problems. The first tool is the Word of God. Daily Bible reading or doing devotionals is crucial to survival in our walk as Christians in a fallen world. The Word of God lays down principals in story form and parables which are simple for our minds to comprehend and easy for our souls to digest. Most Bibles today have concordances, which act as a guide for us if we are looking for something more specific. The Word of God is truth. What we read will seep into the soul.

The second tool is the power of prayer. Making, not taking time to pray each day feeds the soul. First, come into prayer time with praise and thanksgiving, thanking Him for even the worst situation we face at the time. It is thanking Him in the hardest of situations that helps us to know God like no one else. He surely proves His faithfulness when He sees we're not going to behave as a spoiled child and thank Him only when we get what we want. This has a way of humbling us and the Lord honors that. Pray for other's needs before our own, for the Lord already knows what we need before we ask Him. We need to pray in the Spirit, and not watch the clock. We must give Him the best of our time. Praying with our spouses can teach us to pray more effectively. It does wonders to blossom your relationship as well. In such prayer there is such a spiritual intimacy felt with your Heavenly Father and mate at the same time. Thank you

Lord, for that must truly be what He had designed for husband and wife in the beginning.

The third tool is obedience. Serving or doing whatever God lies on our hearts whether we understand or not is true obedience. How many times has God told us to do something, and we disobeyed or sat on it, dragged our heels too long, only to find He sent someone more obedient to do the job? Did we get a little angry or feel guilty perhaps? Obedience is doing what God needs done immediately. Suppose a child were asked to let the dog out to go to the bathroom. Instead, we find that our child waited too long, because he or she played with the dog so long that the dog got excited and wet the tiles in the new kitchen. Was it true obedience to play first and decide without consulting that we had a different time frame in mind in which to do it? We do what we are called or told to do. We do not wait a month, a day, or a year. God has no use for someone who cannot follow a simple command. These people will not be trusted with greater and more important things. Obedience is also for our protection. Why for instance does the Lord say not to have premarital sex? Is it because He knows that you or your future spouse will be injured by the memories of it? What about the diseases today, or the unwanted pregnancies? His guidelines, discipline, and mostly obedience are for our protection. We must listen carefully.

The fourth tool is that we need to walk with confidence in the Lord. What good are our words or our witness if we are wishy-washy?

"Because he who doubts is like a wave of the sea, blown and tossed by the wind. That man should not think he will receive anything from the Lord; he is a double-minded man, unstable in all he does" (James 1: 6-8)

We either know that the Lord is who He says He is, or we do not. No one can be productive for the Lord if they lack the confidence of who they are in Christ.

The last tool is the tool of endurance. If all the other tools are not sharpened and ready, we will not be able endure whatever it is that we will have to face. If we do not spend time reading the Word daily, praying, obeying, or if we lack the confidence of who we are in Christ, then we can forget being able to stand on our two feet to endure, the storm! However, if all our tools are sharp and set in place, we will stand the test. If it is still difficult to endure or it just seems the storm will not blow over, then the process needs to be repeated until it does. Using our tools more often is usually required. There are even times when seeing a counselor, or medical doctor may also be a good idea. No one should ever feel ashamed of getting a little outside help occasionally. God can work through others as well.

Chapter Nine

Treading on Serpents and Scorpions...

"I saw Satan fall like lightning from heaven. I have given you authority to trample on snakes and scorpions and to overcome all the power of the enemy; nothing will harm you" (Luke 10:18&19).

We will have many serpents and scorpions that will come along and try to harm us or keep us from the blessings of God. For some of you these snakes and scorpions could be financial worries, physical afflictions, mental and emotional well - being, spiritual attacks, relationship problems, identity crises, and possibly, addictions. If I have missed an area with which you struggle, you may insert that along with all the others.

Many of these tie in together most of the time. For instance, if a couple struggles to make ends meet; they may each take on two jobs as well as keeping up with children and all their other responsibilities. Sooner or later with or without the Lord's help, someone will burnout. Usually, it is the mother. When your body does not get enough rest, you become more vulnerable for sicknesses to threaten your tent. Already, we can see how the financial and physical immediately interlock. When your body is sick and tired, and you are too consumed with responsibilities; your spiritual life falls by the wayside. We all know and can attest to the fact that when we stop spending time in the Word and or praying with the Father, we begin to struggle mentally and emotionally. This leads to spiritual attacks, relationship problems, addictions and identity crises. What a coincidence! All of these things interlock sooner or later.

God has given us the power to tread upon these things in our life. He promises that these things cannot harm us or destroy us. He didn't however promise that things wouldn't look or feel scary. When we see those dark clouds rolling in, He doesn't want us to tuck tail and run. He wants us to keep our feet firmly planted on the rock; which is Him. The winds will blow and bend us this way and that, but if our roots have grown deep enough, we will not topple over. He shelters you under His wings; in Him can you hide. When I feel really low, I have to reflect upon my favorite scripture.

"For I know the plans that I have for you," declares the Lord, "plans to prosper you and not to harm you, plans to give you a hope and a future. Then you will call upon me and come and pray to me, and I will listen to you. You will seek me and find me when you seek me with all your heart. And I will be found by you," declares the Lord. (Jeremiah 29: 11-14)

Our peace with any situation and ultimately the final out come always comes back to where we are with the Lord. Do we use our tools? Do we truly seek Him with all our hearts? Or is there an ulterior motive hidden inside? Do we walk the walk and not just talk the talk? Do we really love Him and know Him? Are we confident enough in our walk to trust Him with the finality of everything we face, whether it is the answer we want or not? You see, when we get in the way of how God wants to handle things we delay the blessings to come. We also prolong whatever circumstance we struggle with. We need to be focused like a racehorse when he has those blinders on. He can only see straight ahead. There is nothing to distract the horse from the sides. The bit in his mouth steers him, his rider speeds him along, and the blinders keep his eyes on what lies ahead. Ultimately a prize is won. And so will it be with us the day that Christ returns for His people.

"I press on toward the goal to win the prize for which God has called me heavenward in Christ Jesus" (Philippians 3:14).

Living With a System That Fails You

The biggest serpents or scorpions which our little family had to trample on many times unfortunately were government agencies. I have found that the various programs and organizations that are out there to help people sometimes can be the enemy in disguise! For example, there is our governmental system that is supposed to exist to assist in financially helping those who are struggling. Instead, I had found insult after insult of bureaucratic red tape that was altogether unnecessary. I am talking about agencies such as the Social Security Administrative Offices, and Social Services Departments.

Most people cannot humble themselves to go to these places and ask for some type of help. I was one of them. I had been on and off with the WIC program which aids pregnant moms and young children on a limited income by providing milk, cheese, eggs, cereal etc... It was a wonderful source of help having three little mouths to feed. However, when it came to a very critical point in our life with my husband's back injury and his not working, I felt that I needed to get further help from other sources at Social Services. I thank God truly that there are programs that do exist and do help, however, there does need to be a lot of changes implemented in the way that the government deals with the public, and in the manner of how the tons of paperwork is processed.

When you first get up the gumption to go to Social Services, it can be a very humbling experience. You feel everyone is staring you down, and wanting to know if you plan on taking the system for a ride. You see all kinds of people there waiting. No matter your race or creed, you can count on there being hundreds of children whining and crying, waiting to be seen with their parents for about three to four hours. The longer I sat there the more I began stewing inside. It started a war raging inside of me that I almost had no control in handling. I started asking the Lord, "Why am I bothering with all this nonsense!" All I could see were my children's faces. I knew I had to stay for their sake. We needed the food stamps for them, not for us. We needed HEAP for them not for us. If it had just been my husband and I, we could have done without a lot. Everything changes when the innocence of children become involved. So I found myself glued to a chair, gritting my teeth and trying to smile occasionally at the mother next to me who was stuck to her chair, just a gritting and smiling! You've heard of a picking and a grinning! Everyone at Social Services is a gritting and a smiling!

At first when I started going to these places for help, I must confess that I did feel deep down inside that I was a little better than the rest. Maybe I had finer clothes, a nicer car, I kept my body and outward appearance cleaner than most. But God showed me I was not above anyone else in that room. Every person there was facing issues of their own, and most importantly, most of them were lost without the Lord Jesus Christ. There were times when I walked out of places like that feeling like the lowest of lows out there. I felt cheap and slobbish, as if something was wrong with me just because I needed a little assistance for my children's sake. I had been talked down to; told to go get a job etc... I had been outright turned down because the girl handling the interview could not get my information correct the first time I was there in need. I found myself getting angry that I had wasted precious hours filling out paperwork just to sit for hours and to be denied the help I knew my children were rightfully due. The case - worker was less than cordial when she let all my hopes come crashing down that day. She won. We lost. The girl did not do her job right that day. Someone doing their job wrong that day ended up breaking the straw on the camel's back for me. It almost caused me to drive my car into a telephone pole because I saw that appointment as my family's only source of help. When that fell through, and I hadn't seen any kind of miracle for my husband, something inside snapped; I began to lose my mind.

My husband and I were struggling in our marriage at that point in time as well, so it didn't take much to break me that day in the office. It's too bad how one person's mistake could strike a final blow to someone that could cause them to react irrationally. My husband and I would fight over whose responsibility it was to fill out the grueling paperwork and dig up all the proof and then go and sit for three hours, possibly just to be denied. It usually ended up being me. However, that day I came home acting like a crazy woman. At that moment a light went on for my husband as to how much I could and could not handle anymore. He stepped in and tried to make some of the appointments himself which took off a big load for me.

Fighting for Social Security Benefits which we rightly deserved had probably been the biggest struggle of all. When you go up against government agencies you are a nobody; most of the time you do not even exist. It's like David fighting Goliath! When your attorney fails to meet deadlines for you without your knowing about it and you pay the price by losing what you were entitled too, it's an outrage! Not to mention the zillions of times Social Security Disability loss our paperwork and made us go through the procedures over and over again. So when I said earlier that the things that were designed to help are sometimes your biggest enemy, I meant it. I had become our own attorney, judge, and jury. Calling and writing Congressmen, and Senators, is what I did in between schooling my children, massaging my husband's back, and before my music students rolled in for the evening. One day when it would have been so easy to throw in the towel, the Lord helped me to remain calm, and gave me two words over and over. They were Serpents and Scorpions. That is the scripture in Luke that I quoted earlier. These things had been and still are serpents and scorpions to us. We started to trample them and not let them make us fearful, and we told ourselves that the system would not triumph over us because the Lord was in control. Although God is the one in control and He has the final say at how everything ends up, He still gives us the abilities to stand up for our rights and the capabilities to figure and calculate so that we can figure out when something is not adding up logically; and to know when you're being taken.

If people are paying into the system all their lives and something tragic happens as it did to us, then it is only right to get the help you need. The help that exists in these agencies comes from tax payers like you and me. God was going to give the Israelites the Promised Land however, but they were still expected to go in and take the land because it was already occupied. God says that His people perish because of a lack of knowledge. If I had not done some investigating of my own and gone after what we had paid into the system all those years, we would have truly perished by now.

Seasons and Reasons

I believe all the things that have happened to us are all a part of what God has intended for us to be, and these things make up who we are in Christ. Everything we face in this life is for a season. The trials will not last. Sometimes I have been so weak in my faith that the only thing that has gotten me through is just to ponder upon the thought that "it's just a season." My husband's back will not be this way forever! It may never be the way it was before, but it will not get worse, and hopefully it will get better in time. Whatever you face, don't despair, don't worry and don't fear what you think may lie ahead. The Lord wants you to grow from these situations and to learn from them.

He is the potter and you are the clay. Don't forget you are in His hands. What can be more precious than that? A potter must mold and shape the clay so that it doesn't spin out into a huge lopsided lump. A potter takes his time if he wants to do a good job. He cares for his piece of clay, and carefully plans out how beautiful he will make it look. Remember, if He molds us and shapes us, then that means that He has to hold us first. He never lets us go or leaves us unattended.

If I remember correctly from my old school days in Shop Class, we used to do ceramics. I know this may differ somewhat from pottery, but I think the end results are pretty much the same. I remember that the molds needed to be poured. Then they were put into a kiln. Once they came out they would still be a little bit wet. The next step was to scrape off any seams left from the mold itself, and then we would sand them to make them smooth. The pieces were usually quite dusty and would need to be washed down a little. They would then go back to the kiln for a second time. This time when the piece came out, I had to make a decision of whether or not to paint it or just to use a glaze to make it shine. If I decided to just paint it, it would not have a nice shine. Instead I would have to spray it with a protector; and it would be saved from returning to the kiln again. However, if I decided to put a glazed finish on the piece, I would sometimes have to put on two to three coats and it would have to be returned to the kiln. Something very common that can be very disturbing to an impatient potter is when the mold breaks simply from handling, thus possibly losing the whole piece. If this happened, I had to repeat the whole process.

Let's look at this from the Lord's eyes as He is our potter. A mold has to be chosen, you! He takes you as you are, the lump of clay or whatever is being poured into the mold. You are then placed in the fire where you can be purified and hardened. The kiln or fire represents the trials placed in our life to make us grow. Once you are taken from the kiln, your rough spots are smoothed out, for we will not be perfect after coming out of a trial. The Lord will do a little sanding on you and wash away the dust. You've made a lot of progress however, you still just feel like an unfinished product that could never possibly look beautiful after all of this. Because of your progress, it is time to be put back into the fire (kiln) once again. Now you are harder and stronger than before. This procedure had to take place a second time in order for the best and most beautiful part to take place, the painting or glazing. God chooses special brushes to use on you because He knows what will make you or break you in given situations. Some of us need dry brushing, soft brushes, and some of us may need a brush for some specific detailing. If you are painted, you will not be quite as bright as the pieces that are glazed. However, when your beauty is complete, a protectant finish is sprayed upon you and you do not have to face the fire anymore. Those that are glazed to shine more ultimately have to face the fire once more before they are complete. If you feel you do not shine as much as someone else who has a ministry or is in the forefront of the church, don't feel too bad because more than likely those people who hold more of a leadership role, do walk through the fire more often than others.

"Fear not, for I have redeemed you; I have called you by name; you are mine. When you pass through the waters, I will be with you; and when you pass through the rivers, they will not sweep over you. When you walk through the fire (kiln), you will not be burned; the flames will not set you ablaze. For I am the Lord, your God, the Holy One of Israel, your Savior" (Isaiah 43:1-3).

Nothing that we face or walk through is going to destroy us. He walks with us. If He is for us, who or what can stand against us? When you feel tired of being in your season, and you really cannot see the reason for it, just remember Isaiah 63:8,

"Yet, O Lord, you are our Father. We are the clay, you are the potter; we are all the work of your hand."

Don't complain. You would be complaining about something that the Lord was creating. That can be a scary place to be in. Remember what I said earlier, "Every season comes to pass."

A Time for Everything

"There is a time for everything,
and a season for every activity under heaven":

- *a time to be born and a time to die,*
- *a time to plant and a time to uproot,*
- *a time to kill and a time to heal,*
- *a time to tear down and a time to build,*
- *a time to weep and a time to laugh,*
- *a time to mourn and a time to dance,*
- *a time to scatter stones and a time to gather them,*
- *a time to embrace and a time to refrain,*
- *a time to search and a time to give up,*
- *a time to keep and a time to throw away,*
- *a time to tear and a time to mend,*
- *a time to be silent and a time to speak,*
- *a time to love and a time to hate,*
- *a time for war and a time for peace.*

Let us take some of these thoughts and analyze them in order to form a better understanding of the picture before us. The verse is taken from Ecclesiastes 3:1-8. Sometimes people can better understand when we take simple or complicated scripture and compare it to a relative trial or situation to make it a more vivid reality.

It is quite obvious that someone who is born into this world will eventually die (unless the Lord comes back for us). But let us take another look at this, **a time to be born a time to die.**

That can also stand for a ministry, career etc... We are not just talking a physical birth and death. Many of us know and can attest to the fact that ministries are birthed in God's timing and sometimes God will bring a ministry, career to rest by it actually dieing.

My husband and I held two full time ministries from the time we were in our late teens until we were in our mid to late twenties. Both were very successfully used for God's glory, however; we came to a point where things began to change. God was calling us to lay both of those ministries down. He wanted them to die in order for us to be ready to go into a time of rest, a time of peace, and a serious time of new growth. If we had not obeyed and laid down our two ministries, you would not be reading this book today, and many of the events that have happened might not have occurred. Most importantly, we would have missed out on some major blessings as well. It is painful to let something die, especially if it has been a dream of yours, but it always pays off walking in God's path, not our own.

Sometimes in a case of a ministry, the ministry itself may not die, but you are called to die to it. Others may be brought in to fill your shoes, which is difficult to accept especially when you don't see where God is leading you next. That was the way it was for us. Sometimes that ministry goes on forever and you will question why you were pulled from it especially when there was no place left to go. Don't make that your focus. Just feel proud to know you were privileged to have had a part in making that ministry what it is or was. All the things we die to are a gain to us for they served as a time of training and experience for what God has for us next, as well as being able to help and bless those in the process.

A time to plant and a time to uproot. God plants us in a situation, job, or a ministry because he knows where we will be most effective. He knows our capabilities, he even knows the people that we will be able to minister too even if it is not a ministry we're talking about. For example, we can minister to many people just by a trial that we are walking through and how they see us handling it. Do we trust in the Lord? Do we whine and cry about every little upset? Do we hold ourselves with grace and dignity? Are we impatient and easily angered when things don't seem to let up? How we handle situations can be just as much a witness to others as a ministry itself. If they see you facing a hardship and think to themselves, "Oh my gosh! I'd go nuts by now if that were me!" Yet they see how strong you've stayed in your faith that has just proven to them that God will take them through the worst possible situation and eventually take them from the valley and place them on the mountaintop.

Now if we think of our gardens, even a kindergartner will tell you what gets planted will be dug up. Everything gets uprooted at some point in time. God planted my husband and me into those two ministries where we were able to do a lot of good for the Lord and receive a lot of experience, but he also said, "It's time to move on now." We were being uprooted when we did not want to be. Let me tell you it hurt, it was very unpleasant. We felt so abandoned and foolish because everyone else saw our actions as being irresponsible. When we do not see our path in life marked out before us and suddenly we are uprooted from where we were for quite a long time, it is very upsetting. About five years down the road we began to see why God had done what he did. Through that time we received counsel from a former pastor, through that time who encouraged us to listen and to heed God's voice. I'm glad we did.

God spoke to me when we were struggling with laying it all down, and told me some things that He was going to do. We were feeling burned out and He was calling us to time of rest. He also told me we were going to be getting our new home that we had been dreaming about. He also told me we would have another child. It was more difficult for my husband than it was for me to lay everything down. It wasn't easy for me, but I had peace. My husband didn't until we pressed into the Lord and I was able to share with him what I felt the Lord was saying to me. I want you to know that everything God told me He was going to do after our uprooting took place, happened in exactly the same order. It felt good knowing I had heard God right, and that all of it came to pass. These seasons do not come to stay. The time of resting in Him gave us the spiritual growth and strength to face what lie ahead when our new house and baby came. This proved to be the greatest trial yet, and we still have not completely walked out of the fire. This of course was when my husband broke his back six months after the new house went up and while I was six months pregnant with our third child.

Because my husband could no longer work, God placed us back into one of the ministries he had pulled us from originally, and He also gave my husband back his music ministry even though it was with a different band. The experience now that we have had because we obeyed and allowed God to take our family through the fire is unbelievable. We are so much better equipped now for the new places God has called us to walk because of the time of rest He gave us. There was much learning and growing spiritually that happened as we were called from the busyness of ministry to the solitude of His restful arms. Now *we* are the leaders instead of being the ones trained in that area, *we* are the ones responsible for it all and I love it because God has been burning that desire in our hearts for a long time and has been placing over time, leadership qualities upon us.

My husband, my sixteen year old, and I play on the praise team as well. My husband was asked to serve as an elder of the church which was a real honor. There was a shift in responsibilities that needed to take place as well as the spiritual growth required and lessons of suffering to be learned in order for us to fill the positions we were called too. My husband is in his sophomore year of college studying ministry and music which is part of the call that he feels urged to answer. Though we still have not come into the fullness of what we believe God is really calling us too, we remain faithful where we have been planted because we know that when you are found faithful in the little things, God will put you in charge of bigger things.

When we were unsure of ourselves or when we questioned whether or not we heard God's voice right, He always made sure to give us a sign that it was all okay. One of the signs He showed me had absolutely everything to do with what we're talking about; being uprooted. I went to hear a woman speak at our church one evening. What did she talk about? She proceeded to do a demonstration of transplanting a plant she already had grown. She proceeded to explain that sometimes God will uproot us from where we are because He knows that in the long run if He takes us out of the pot that is getting too cramped, then growth will not be hindered. By placing us in a bigger pot with fresh soil our roots will be able to spread out further and become stronger. This in turn will help in producing beautiful fruit.

A time to kill and a time to heal. There comes a time when we need to kill the old man. What do I mean? I don't mean to go find some 'ole geezer and take him out! The old man is the old you that kept you enslaved to sin for so long. Just like when I stayed in a state of anger and unforgiveness for so long. It changed me into someone my family did not even recognize anymore. Some of us have lived a really wild and rebellious life. Some of us have experimented a little bit with different things but never harmed anyone, and some of us were raised in the church our whole lives and led a life that was pretty clean, a life with very few bumps in the road. Regardless of what kind of life you have led, or are leading today, every human being needs to be in touch with the Creator. We can't be close to the Father when sin is so prevalent in our lives. A wall immediately will go up between you and the Lord, and it will be nearly impossible to grow. We need to fall on our knees and recognize that we are sinners. Even though we may not have murdered someone, or had an affair, or dealt drugs, sin is sin, and we all need to bury the old self so that the new self can emerge and flourish in changed life. God's Word says in 2 Corinthians 5:17,

"Therefore, if anyone is in Christ, he is a new creation; the old has gone, the new has come!"

That new self when we come to know the Father as our Lord and Savior needs some gentle care. It needs to be fed milk like an infant who is not old enough to eat solids yet. So is it the same when you're a baby Christian. You need to heal and toss out the baggage as you begin to grow or your growing will come to a stand still.

A time to tear down and a time to build. Sometimes there are things in our lives that can destroy us or cause us to fall away from the Lord. Sometimes we may have to make ourselves get out of relationships that will only cause havoc in our lives and put us at odds with our Heavenly Father. Sometimes when the old man has been destroyed, it's not as easy for the evidence left behind by the old man to be destroyed. Sometimes our flesh is so much stronger than our new self (Spirit) that we still find our addictions and bad habits still lying around. Get rid of anything that hinders you.

"Therefore, since we are surrounded by such a great cloud of witnesses, let us throw off everything that hinders and the sin that so easily entangles, and let us run with perseverance the race marked out for us. Let us fix our eyes on Jesus, the author and perfector of our faith, who for the joy set before him endured the cross, scorning its shame, and sat sown at the right hand of the throne of God," (Hebrews 12:1-2).

You need to work on building a new life, new relationships with people who have been there and can give you the support you need. God will build a new you, new relationships, careers, and new ministries as well.

A time to weep and a time to laugh. Some of us have walked a harder road than others. For instance, some grow up being abused, abandoned, laughed at, or just plain neglected. Others have it easier than others who seem to struggle with one thing after another. However, even these people will have an occasional hurdle to jump over. There is a time to grieve about our misfortunes; however, God does not want us to waste the life He intended to use for good, instead going 'round and 'round the same issues that cause us great pain. Let Him make you strong. Begin to find something to be happy about. If you can't think of anything, then perhaps you need to begin to be glad that you can just make the decision and say, "I'm going to get help with these issues I can't seem to get past on my own, and I'm going to be happy again, because I'm worth it!" The bible says in Proverbs 17:22,

"A cheerful heart is good medicine, but a crushed spirit dries up the bones."

Learn to laugh. When it says, He will turn your mourning into dancing basically means don't waste your life grieving over the loss of a loved one to the point of not moving on with your life or shutting yourself off from family and friends to the extent that you stop living. Maybe you're not grieving the loss of someone but rather the loss of a job, a pet, a ministry, or a relationship. God wants us to grieve, yes! However, He offers healing and does not want us to destroy ourselves with self pity or to shut ourselves off from His blessings and the work that He has for us to do. You may have to make yourself be joyful, shout to the Lord for joy and yes, even set your feet to dancing for the good that still exists. When you look hard enough, you can find that joy. Something extraordinary happens when you force yourself to worship, to dance before Him or bow on bended knee, or even extend your helping hand to someone in need. God meets you there and things begin to turn around. I've experienced this first hand. Your attitude slowly begins to change, and your outlook on life does not seem so bleak anymore. You begin to feel the hope that you were longing to feel once again or for some for the first time. If you are stuck in a depressed mode such as I have experienced, you MUST put in a worship CD. That has many times been the life saver for me. When you are so distraught that you can't pray, read the Word, or even function, worship music has a way of calming your spirit, and causing you to rise up out of that slump.

We can take each of the following verses and continue to compare it with the problems we face each day and know that everything happens for a reason, and that trials will not last forever. We can also learn from Ecclesiastes 9:2-3,

"All share a common destiny-the righteous and the wicked, the good and the bad, the clean and the unclean, those who offer sacrifices and those who do not. As it is with the good man, so with the sinner; as it is with those who take oaths, so with those who are afraid to take them. This is the evil in everything that happens under the sun: The same destiny overtakes all."

"He causes his sun to rise on the evil and the good, and sends rain on the righteous and the unrighteous" (Matthew 5:45).

These scriptures confirm one another. They state that it just does not matter whether we know God or not, we are not always spared tragedies, sickness, disease, or very difficult trials. However, when we choose to walk with God, when we choose to press into Him, His Word says this:

"And we know that in all things God works for the good of those who love him, and have been called according to his purpose," (Rom. 8:28).

The only comfort and assurance that we will have getting through our difficulties even *if* we are righteous and even *if* we have always obeyed is the fact that the ones who walk with God will have His help to get us through the trials. We become stronger for it, our characters are sharpened and God will use us for His glory, and as an example that will shine to all.

Those that face the same difficulties but choose not to walk with Him will end up in destruction, they do not walk in the assurance that they will not drown in the waters or be burned in the fire. You see, God promises his children this:

"When you pass through the water, I will be with you; and when you pass through the rivers, they will not sweep over you. When you walk through the fire, you will not be burned; the flames will not set you ablaze. For I am the Lord, your God, the Holy One of Israel, your Savior," (Isaiah 43:2&3).

Don't try to figure out what He's doing through it all either. You will drive yourself mad. He also says this,

"For my thoughts are not your thoughts, neither are your ways my ways," declares the Lord. "As the heavens are higher than the earth, so are my ways higher than your ways and my thoughts than your thoughts," (Isaiah 55:8&9).

Because of our carnal minds we tend to think, "God, if you would just do it this way." Or, we just decide to step to the right or left without really hearing clearly from Him before hand, thinking we have it all figured out that this must be what He's thinking, and then we just go. The trouble is that we end up in left field, missing the mark and the blessings along the way. Put your faith and trust in the one who created you and the one who knows you best.

Trials will come and go. We will all face them. Yes, we all at some point in time go through a very trying time, and just when you feel that you have come through one and survived, another one seems to roll in. Did you ever find yourself thinking this? "Isn't there something more to this Christian life than just suffering all the time?" Or, "I might as well just turn around and live the life of the non believer since they seem to just breeze their way through life!" Why work so hard to always do the right thing, to try to be happy, to never complain, to never worry, to always turn the other cheek, and let's not forget the BIG one, to always forgive when we don't feel it inside? I've said all of these at one point or another.

It would be easy to say, "That's it, I'm done! God, if you can't or won't bring me out of this now, then I'm walking out, I'm finished, goodbye." I've felt my life spinning hopelessly out of control even though I pray, talk with God, read the Word, fellowship with others, have a good marriage and family support. The stress can still be so overwhelming that you want to quit! You lose patience with the dog, co-workers, employer, spouse, and children. That is when you must draw the line, and say to yourself I've got to make some choices here. Sometimes, especially for women, we need to have some counseling. I've been there too. I can't tell you how healing it is to find a good Christian counselor who will listen objectively. You can unload all the garbage and not have to worry about stressing out someone else you love.

It is also beneficial to cut down the workload whether your workload is a stay at home mom, or a professional. Taking a cut in your income because you had to make some cutbacks seems devastating; however, you can learn to adjust especially if it is just for a season. Ask yourself this: Can you live a little while with a little less money, or a little less sanity? It becomes pretty clear, doesn't it? When your body is under stress it affects every part of your being. Sometimes we adjust to a high stress life and don't realize it anymore until it is too late. That is what happened to me. Stress can be like a semi coming on full speed and crashing because the driver didn't read the danger signs and slow down earlier. If you are not careful in detecting the warning signs that your body is showing you, you crash and burn. Stress can do horrible things and especially cause a lot of hormonal problems for women as if we didn't have enough problems. Sometimes the recovery after you crash can take twice as long because you didn't pay attention to the warning signs.

Another good thing to try to do if you're under a lot of stress is to find time to do something that you enjoy such as horseback riding, skiing, or painting. My outlet was to start figure skating lessons at the age of thirty. It's been a way of escape and a time to fulfill a life long dream. Although I know I will never make the Olympics or even make a career of it, I can say that I made an attempt to fulfill a life long dream. I've always wanted to skate to music like all the skaters I have admired over the years. I have even dreamed that I was an accomplished skater just flying over the ice and spinning. It feels so real when I have those dreams. I feel so free from all my struggles and fears and stress. Then I wake up and the awful realization hits me that I am not that accomplished skater in my dreams, and that another day I will face the fact that my husband still lives in pain, and finances are tight, and that I will still have my responsibilities as well as my husband's to fulfill as well as teach, work, and hold down a full time ministry. I do however, get up out of bed and feel charged and excited to hit the ice again. I whisper to myself that someday I will accomplish the things I have always wanted to try on the ice. It may never happen, but I am just having fun with it regardless. I may never be a Tara Lipinski, but I will be myself, refined from the fire (the trials of life), and able to express all that I have been through as I breeze over the ice, skating my heart out.

No matter what it takes, pace yourself in life. Do not be too anxious for trials to pass because sometimes when we walk out of a trial we are left wondering, okay now what? Sometimes we find ourselves fantasizing about how wonderful life is going to be once this season passes. Let me share with you that although in some ways things lighten up and seem great, ahead of you will lay new decisions. Sometimes a whole new life such as career changes, ministry changes are suddenly upon you. You realize that some of the storm you just walked through and the areas you grew in are now what have prepared you for the decisions that lie ahead. Usually a new person emerges. You can feel energized because in some ways life has gotten easier, but there still lies some fear about this new path you are on. You became so used to the fire and always falling on your knees in need of God's rescue, to all of a sudden, being as free as a bird who was just let out of his cage. It is normal in some strange way to feel abandoned, empty, and completely insane or guilty for being free from what you had been walking in for so long. Why, some of you ask? It is because if you have ever walked through the fire, especially for any length of time, there is a closeness that you feel to your Father that is unexplainable. When that season is over, it is as if He's cut you loose from what has bogged you down for so long, that you stand there wanting to be told or instructed as to what to do next. We were never promised a rose garden however, it can be the sweetest place to be in the arms of your Savior who leads you to grace.

Chapter Ten

"I Can Conquer the World"

Because a man hung on a tree,
I have every reason to be free.
I didn't even know his name,
But someone said He loved me just the same.
I can conquer the world.

I was filling my life with everything
Except the things that happiness brings
Selfishness, jealousy, envy and strife,
No wonder I never had any peace in life.
I can conquer the world.

Things spin out of control; I can't go on anymore,
Where do I begin, why can't it be like before?
Do I curl up and die, do I run the other way?
Is this a game I really want to play?
I can conquer the world.

There are days when I am feeling strong,
Then a day creeps up I ask myself, "What's wrong?"
"Get a grip, what's the matter with you?"
Then that's when I hear the evil one say,
"You're falling apart; you'll not survive another day"
I will conquer the world.

I am not crazy, just stressed out of my mind,
I can hear the enemy as he tries to strike me blind,
From the things I know to be true from the Father above,
It's His mercy, grace, and peace but mostly it's His love,
That is why I can say,
I will conquer the world.

Without His daily guidance in my life,
I would have never survived the craziness, all the strife,
I give Him all the glory for what's been birthed in me,
All the struggles, the things that broke me down,
I want all to see,
That they too can conquer the world.

    The only way that we can keep the healthy, mental attitude that we can conquer the world is by staying close to the Father. If we do not spend time in the Word, or in prayer, we will become weak. When obstacles are thrown at our feet, suddenly we cannot see our way around them. If we haven't tucked away God's Word in our hearts, how will we be able to overcome? How will we be able to hold onto any happiness or peace in our life?

    Imagine that you are following a path in the woods. You may know where approximately you will end up, maybe you don't, and maybe it is completely an adventure. You make sure you are dressed appropriately. You have even packed some snacks to feed your ever, empty pit that seems to scream out to you to feed it every half an hour. Not only are you prepared for any kind of weather, but you are prepared with the right kind of footgear, first aid kit, and a survival knife as well.

    As you begin your journey, you notice the storm clouds rolling in. The forecast did not call for this, but you came prepared…you think. An hour into your journey you realize the one thing you did forget was bug repellant. Fifty mosquito bites later it begins to pour, and you decide to take cover and quiet that stomach of yours. After your snack you feel revived and satisfied. You feel as if you could conquer the world. It is still pouring which in a way is your only escape from the terribly hungry bugs that need to seek shelter themselves. You brought a slicker and even an umbrella to weather the storm. However, because of the lightning now getting closer with every heartbeat you decide it best to seek out some type of cave. Your thoughts are to get out of harm's way not thinking you would be put in further danger. After another mile of mud and cuts and bruises, you manage to find X marks the spot on the map you have. A dark cave covered by all kinds of brush and poison ivy. Great! Like the last thing you need is to trip and fall into the deadly hands of that poisonous plant! You pull your survival knife and quickly begin cutting away at some of the brush hoping to make a clean entrance away from the ivy. After your knife slips out of your hand and into the river below, you suddenly feel as if someone has put a hex on your trip. You are distraught, scared and shivering from the cold rain. Entering this dark cave is about the worst it can get. Your imagination begins to run wild. Your stomach seems to remind you that when all else fails eat! The rock to the right begins to look like it can offer you some much needed rest. Half way into your granola bar, you see the whites of the eyes of some unknown creature lurking in the cave with you. As it approaches you with its hungry cries you notice that it is a growing cub probably with a very curious and protective mama following close behind. A growing cub means not this cute little cuddly baby bear. Rather one who has approached their maximum size before entering into Mama Bear, Papa Bear stage. Now that all three are observing you with hungry eyes, you remember your knife dropping down into the ravine below. Quickly, you pull out all the food you packed and throw it out as a smorgasbord before them, thus allowing you to make a quick exit from the only place for miles that could shelter you.

Five hundred yards out you can tell the company you had just parted with wants companionship, or just something more to eat. Now the greatest feat is yet to come. With blistered feet, and sore hands, you decide to take the short wide path on the map because it has less brush to worry about. Before you make the turn off for your newly found path in the opposite direction, you decide to throw out those last two snacks you hoarded to deter the bear.

The lightning has subsided and the rain has let up however, it has poured so hard and long that your journey was becoming long and hard. Although there is less brush now, you realize that you are way out in the open and very exposed and vulnerable. Everything has this sort of eerie quietness. The only thing you can hear is your bottomless pit again. Out of luck there! You stopped to rest and realized how out of shape you are. You think maybe if you had conditioned yourself better, you would have been more prepared and not as exhausted.

The point is you need to be conditioning yourself spiritually and most importantly, daily. Why? Everyone who is busy wonders why it is so important to start the day in the Word or in prayer and better yet, both. This is why. You do not know what card will be dealt to you each and every day. It is not just you that is dealt a card everyday but it is everyone you care about as well. For example: a best friend who has cancer, a father-in-law who's losing his sight or a child who's lost a limb. The list goes on and on. We all have stories to tell. If you wake up each and every day without spending time with the Lord, there may come a day when you or your loved one has been given a raw deal. Are you going to be prepared to cope with what has been dealt to you? Not just for the purpose of how you are going to handle it, but most importantly, how you will be able to minister to someone else that is hurting. I truly feel that being fed daily and talking with God daily gives you some kind of preparation for the things that lie just around the corner that we don't ever expect will touch us or someone we love.

Sometimes a scripture you've read on Wednesday will not mean anything until Saturday, or next Wednesday. It is God's way of preparing us for battle, and His way of making us somewhat strong as we enter the desert areas of our lives. What always gave me comfort when I felt I was in the desert never to come out was the fact that the Holy Spirit led Jesus into the wilderness. Let's look at Matthew chapter four. I already stated that the Holy Spirit led Jesus into the wilderness to be tempted by the Devil. Now let us dig into this a little further.

Jesus was fasting. After John baptized him, he got up and was led to the wilderness. There was no more eating from that point on for forty days and nights. Remember how our stomach cries every half an hour to eat? Imagine forty days and nights with nothing to eat. It was not as if He were in the comfort of His own home, where He could relax when He became fatigued from not eating. I imagine you could develop a nasty headache going without food that long. Now think about the climate in that part of the world. A temperature reaching probably in the 100's easily and even hotter in the savannas and desert lands. He was out there alone, hungry, fatigued, and surely not in the best physical condition. In the evenings the temperature could have dropped drastically, leaving him cold with nothing to cover up with.

The temptations begin with Jesus already being hungry. Now how many of us can attest to the fact that when we are hungry, people better get out of our way. Don't distract us with this or that; keep your questions and stories brief 'cause we have got to find us some food. Has that ever happened to you? Your children are babbling something but you've got a one track mind…FOOD! I do not imagine that Jesus was in the mood for company from the number one enemy of His Father. He was not in the mood to be tempted either; I guarantee it! Notice that the Devil's first attack on Jesus was where Jesus' weakness was at the time, HUNGER! The Devil tempts Jesus with stones that could be turned into a lovely loaf of bread to satisfy his hunger. Jesus fought Satan every time with scripture. This is why we need to know the Word of God. Jesus gave us an example in this chapter. We are to live by this standard. We need to fight with the Word of God. In order to do this, you have to do some serious digesting of the Bible. Next, Satan came after Jesus to try and instill doubt into him. Satan tells Jesus, "If you are the Son of God, then throw yourself down." He proceeds to tell him that his Father would send angels to catch him so He wouldn't strike a rock. By saying this to the Son of God, Satan hoped in Jesus' weakness to make him feel the need to prove who He really was by jumping. Notice Satan used words that God used. Satan can come after us with God's own word and take it out of context. What Satan was really doing was testing God and hoping that the Son of God would do the same. Satan erred in doing so because Jesus refuted the scripture taken out of context and used another one right back on him. Do not test the Lord your God. Now the third time Jesus was tempted, He must have been really in rough shape and extremely exhausted by then. Satan thinks now that Jesus has about had it, that Jesus would surely want to prove Himself by now. He knew that with all the good Jesus was there to do on earth even though His ministry had just begun, that people wouldn't appreciate who He really was. Everyone wants to be recognized for something that they have accomplished, even if it is just a tiny bit. Satan tried to make Jesus desire the praise of man, the recognition of man, the acceptance of man. Instead, they both knew that Jesus would be humble and that His kingdom would not be of that world, and He would ultimately not be accepted by man. Satan made the nations of the world look very appealing and desirable however, Jesus says, "Get out of here, Satan!" Jesus proceeds to fight him off with scripture one last time. "You must worship the Lord your God; serve only Him." What is remarkable here is that Jesus told him plain and simple, "GET!"

Do not even entertain thoughts that the Devil puts in your head. Stop them before you can even dwell on anything. Know the Word of God before something comes your way and you can't find the strength to get through it. Know and understand that when you walk with God He will lead you through the wilderness. You must be willing to follow. Just take His hand and let Him lead. He will lead you safely through. That scripture ends like this:

"And the angels came and ministered to him."

Can you just picture what went on there? Did Jesus collapse? Did He cry out in frustration? Did He scream out, "Father, help me?" Did the angels feed Him? Did they care for any bruises or cuts He may have gotten roaming in the wilderness that long? Did they just stay with Him and guide Him safely home? We could ask question after question. The point is it doesn't matter really. The angels took care of Him regardless. His every need was met, and He passed the test. He must have been tempted so much harder than we. Think of it, He is the Son of God. Satan would have tried super hard to knock Him down because that would have totally destroyed God's whole plan of salvation. Everything would have been over with at that point.

Sometimes we feel heavily attacked; however, I think it's small in comparison to what Jesus endured. He fasted as well. When you fast, for forty days and nights, it has a way of putting your back against the wall and leaving you no other option but to press in good and hard to the Lord. He knows you are serious and mean business by sacrificing so much. That is when you really begin to see your prayers answered. Some of us fast only one meal, or do just a juice fast. There are many different kinds of ways that fasts have been done. Nothing was quite the same as forty days and nights. I'm not by any means suggesting that you do a fast such as Jesus had done. I'm just saying that some type of fast would really be pressing in to answers that the Lord has for you. I firmly believe that is what the Lord is speaking about in Jeremiah 29:11-14. The Lord states that when you seek me earnestly (fasting and prayer) you will find me.

Chapter Eleven

The Exodus

We all want to get (exit) out of our problems. Sometimes when we struggle with different circumstances in our lives it is somehow comforting to know someone else has walked there before. Not that we wish people the pain of our struggles, but when you are really hurting sometimes the only comfort is knowing that you are not the only one in the world who has faced problems. Though some of our struggles are very similar to what someone else is going through each problem still differs a little bit especially in the way it affects each person. Some people are strong no matter what, some are easily frustrated, some panic, some get depressed, some are easily wounded, and some just crumble at the littlest thing. Why? We are all unique.

"For you created my inmost being; you knit me together in my mother's womb. I praise you because I am fearfully and wonderfully made; your works are wonderful, I know that full well. My frame was not hidden from you when I was made in the secret place. When I was woven together in the depths of the earth, your eyes saw my unformed body. All the days ordained for me were written in your book before one of them came to be."

We were all made with different characteristics, personalities and qualities. Naturally, it is a given we will not handle stress exactly the same. That is okay. We should not compare ourselves to Tom or Sally. Tom and Sally are not YOU! No matter how we look at it they will always handle things differently. We need to look to the one who created us; who knows us like a book. He will show us how to handle a given situation and I have also found that when we need His grace it will be given to us. Think of a little child. There are children who have real passive personalities, and ones who are very strong willed. Both children will handle situations as differently as night and day. If you tell a passive child that it is time to put the Nintendo up, he might give a little sigh because his fun is coming to an end. A majority of the time, they are quick to obey, and very eager to please you. The strong willed child will react far more dramatically. He will get angry, say a few choice words, stick his tongue out, kick and throw a tantrum on the floor, and possibly break the Nintendo system. How can they be so different? You may laugh but it is not funny to the parent who has to constantly battle these differences day in and day out several times a day. I have been there. Obviously I love it more when one of my children cooperates rather than when he kicks and fights me all the way. I would guess it would be an accurate assumption if I were to say that the Lord probably feels the same about His children.

I am raising a passive child, a strong willed child and one who is a mix of both. I can say from experience that people immediately think when they see a strong willed child that he is naughty, trouble, and that he will never amount to anything. I cannot tell you how many times people have criticized my child right in front of him just because of the stereotype that all strong willed children have ADD. They are labeled even within family members and congregations. What I have found is this. God will still use these different temperaments in a positive way. For instance, strong willed children have stood strong against peer pressure. Sometimes the passive children go along with the crowd, and are easily influenced. Strong willed children can be more aggressive in sharing the gospel with their friends. Passive children are not real bold, but they know right from wrong and do a good job standing their ground. Yes! It is true that most of the time strong willed children swing into rebelliousness, and the passive children tend to obey and not get into a lot of trouble. However, with strong discipline and godly rearing these attributes good and bad will be channeled in a positive direction and you will begin to reap the benefits of all your hard work in childrearing. Whatever the strong willed child does he does with everything he's got. For example, even when my son gets sick, it is traumatic. "I hate this!" He makes all kinds of screeches and wails of disapproval from this sickness that has invaded his body. When he sleeps after being on the go all day, he sleeps HARD! An earthquake could shake him out of his bed and he would still keep on sleeping. When he is playing and writing music on his keyboard he plays hard; sings with all his might. There are positive and negatives that coincide with both personalities. People very seldom or never see the positive traits in a strong willed person.

For instance, let us take a look at Peter. When Jesus first met Peter he was doing what he did best, fishing. This was Peter's livelihood. This is how he fed his family and made a living. Luke chapter five tells the story well. After a hard day and evening of fishing and being unsuccessful, Peter and his crew decided to pack it up and call it a day. By the way, it was probably done in frustration and discouragement as well. Jesus saw this as a great opportunity to reach a strong hard man. Jesus gets into Peter's boat and asks him to put out from the shore a little bit. Peter does and Jesus begins to teach the people. When Jesus finished, and said to Peter, "Put out into deep water, and let down the nets for a catch." Peter replies, "Master, we've worked hard all night and haven't caught a thing." Peter has to get the last word in; has to make his point known. That is part of the strong willed nature. They cannot do something when asked without making a scene or getting the last word in. Here comes passive Jesus telling him to go out deeper for a catch. Something happens when God is able to get hold of a strong willed person. They may have some rough edges like the rest of us however, what does Peter say to Jesus? "But because you say so, I will let down the nets." God has a way of making that stubbornness become obedience.

Let's take another quick look at how Jesus saw Peter's strength. In Matthew 16:16 it says, Jesus asks Peter, "Who do you say I am?" Peter answered, "You are the Christ, the Son of the Living God." Jesus replied, "Blessed are you, Simon son of Jonah, for this was not revealed to you by man, but by my Father in Heaven. And I tell you that you Peter are a rock, and on this rock I will build my church, and the gates of Hades will not overcome it." Jesus admired Peter's strength and boldness. Jesus built His church upon that. My point in all of this is to show you that strong willed people are stereotyped, and do have very good qualities if they are channeled in the right direction. God needs all types of people to do His work. Let us now look at a passive personality and see how God decides to use Him as well.

Let's take a close look at Moses. Some of us think of Moses as being strong because he was raised under the Egyptians and was cruel to his own people before he found out who he really was. If we look closely, we will find that despite his physical features, his personality was not one of a strong willed nature. If we take a look at Exodus 3: 11, we will see the lack of confidence in Moses. After God tells him to go to Pharaoh Moses says, "Who am I, that I should go to Pharaoh and bring the Israelites out of Egypt?" God states that He will be with Moses. God even reassures Moses with a sign. Moses turns to God again and says, "Suppose I go to the Israelites and say to them, 'The God of your fathers has sent me to you,' and they ask me, 'What is his name?' Then what shall I tell them?" God in turn says, "I AM WHO I AM." This doubting God business, fear and dread, lack of confidence, whatever you want to call it in Moses goes on and on. Moses again questions the Lord in chapter four verse one. "What if they do not believe me or listen to me and say, 'The Lord did not appear to you'?" Eventually God's anger burns towards Moses. Moses was slow in speech, which was one of his fears, so God ends up saying that He will send

Moses's brother Aaron to do the talking. After this, Moses does what God commands without question. If Moses had been of a strong willed nature he would have told God, "No way!" He did not however, and he did not obey immediately either. With God's encouragement, Moses obeyed. God used both Peter and Moses mightily. They changed the lives of many people and still impact Christians today.

Now let us take a look at a people as a whole to see how they reacted to what God required of them. Let us look at the Israelites. They did not do too badly in the beginning when God sent Moses and Aaron to tell them to pack up, to use bread with no yeast, and to take gold and possessions from the Egyptians. Why did they not have a problem obeying in the beginning? They did not have a problem listening to the Lord then because they were so distraught about their oppression in Egypt that they were desperate to do anything to escape the bondage. Once they walked out of their slavery, the problems arose. They second guessed the Lord and the appointed one God had placed in charge, Moses. They doubted, and began to borrow trouble before trouble ever came. For example, they were fearful that the Egyptians were going to hunt them down like animals, and they began to complain about their hunger. They became a very angry, whiny people. They said things to Moses such as, "Why did you bring us out here to die?" and, "At least if we had stayed in Egypt, we would have had full bellies!" God could not believe what He was hearing.

> "Moses heard all the families standing in front of their tents weeping, and the Lord became extremely angry. Moses was also very aggravated" (Numbers 11:10).

The problem here is the same with us when we go through our own struggles. The fact is that God can see the way through the problem when we cannot. God knows that even though what we walk through is not easy, He alone has everything under control. He knows that He is not going to abandon us and leave us out there fending for ourselves. He has every intention of getting us through with blessings. We on the other hand begin to fear, doubt and whine and complain because suddenly we are walking into new territory.

Even though the Egyptians were freed and they should have been thankful, it was still a difficult thing leaving all they knew and lived for, for years. Now that may sound strange however, some things were better in their slavery than they were in the wilderness. In Egypt they had full bellies, and never had to pay for their food. They had shelter every night after slaving all day long. In the wilderness, all they had was manna to eat until God sent them the quail. Even then He was so angry with them that He caused a severe plague to break out among them after they began eating. God would have gladly sent them quail perhaps if they have said, "God, we thank you for the many ways you have blessed us out here and especially for our freedom. Lord if we have found favor in your eyes, we pray that you will bless us and send us some meat to eat at least for our children's sake." They did not do that. Instead they became angry and rebellious in their attitudes and hearts. What's worse is that they began to long for the old days in Egypt just because their bellies and their children's bellies were getting the best of them. God would have answered their humble prayer. They chose not to believe God for what they needed let alone for what they wanted. How many times do we long for the way things used to be just because we are growing weary in the trial we walk?

God gives us many steps in a certain direction. The first thing we may be asked to do may be easier than the second step and so on. The first steps for the Israelites were easy, pack up and leave. The next step was difficult. They did not know where they were going, where they would sleep, or what they would eat. They endured the cries of their children, a fact which must have pained them greatly and made them weary. To hear that your child was hungry and thirsty and that they were tired from the heat and the journey would pull at your heart strings and cause you to break under the pressure. But you see God saw that it was going to be okay, they did not. They did not trust and believe and that frustrated the Lord. He set them free as He said and He could not see why they would not believe Him the rest of the way.

Since my husband's injury, we have lost the breadwinner of the family. Financially it has been overwhelming. My husband has lost a lot in his abilities to do the things he once could. We constantly battle the fear of not knowing what lies ahead for our family. Will he ever work again? Will he ever know life without pain? Our lives since this injury have patterned the lives of the Israelites so much. We have turned our struggles into Bible lessons for our children and they see first hand how God alone answers prayer and how He still provides. When you ask yourself these similar questions, you too will find that just as sure as the Israelites were unsure so are you. Just as sure as the Israelites were scared, angry, confused, filled with doubt, and absolutely walked in blind faith not knowing where they would be led next, you can be sure that God <u>WILL</u> deliver you out of what you are facing as well. Will He totally rescue you from it all? He will rescue you, but He knows that in order for you to grow and mature, you must face uncertainties, and circumstances that put your back against the wall until there is nowhere to turn but to Him.

There were times when our backs were against the wall, when our cupboards were completely empty and there was no money in sight. The kids would whine and complain that there was nothing to eat, obviously oblivious to our situation. I remembered feeling like the Israelite parents who must have endured the cries of their hungry children time and again. I felt their frustration, their abandonment, and their fears of what are we going to do if.... What we chose to do was different from the Israelites because we learned from their stories. We chose to sit as a family and pray. We told the kids that mommy and daddy did not have money to buy groceries, and that God already knew our need but that we were going to agree and ask God to provide any way He saw fit. Those were hard, scary, and tearful times for us all. We tried to hide our financial troubles from the children but when they opened the cupboards there was no lying about why there was nothing to eat. Afterward we would pray as a family, and God remained true. Somehow a bill would not be quite as high as anticipated, or we would receive gift certificates for groceries, or even have them delivered to our front door. No one on earth knew on those occasions that our cupboards were bare, but God did and He put it on someone's heart to help. I am not saying that we were never angry like the Israelites, or wanted to rebel out of spite that we were dealt this situation and not delivered from it when we wanted to be, because we did experience those things as well. We did find though that we walked through things quicker and with more grace when we prayed, and did not give up hope. Did you know that it says in God's word that the Israelites's stay in the wilderness was prolonged because of their whining and crying?

Chapter Twelve

The Lifeless Shoes...

If anything ever resembled the vivaciousness of life it would have to be the shoe. Our shoes are reminders of the objects that fill them, and everything that person did or stood for. Shoes have been worn in gardens, amusement parks, churches, workforce, school, shopping and the list goes on. We even have our favorites to choose from. The ones that equip us better and better suit our need. For example; a soccer game, a game of golf, or a stroll down the road on a quiet afternoon. How about our dress shoes we save for special occasions or the frumpy, tattered, holey ones that we just cannot part with? It's funny the importance that shoes have in our lives. You can tell a lot about a person by the shoes they wear. You can tell if that person has flamboyancy for life, or if they are content just to lounge around the house. Some of us really wear our shoes out. Good ones, old ones, we just are so full of action and life that every time we turn around we need a new pair.

There is one type of shoe in particular that I want to talk about, and that is the Lifeless Shoe. The Lifeless Shoe symbolizes the shoe that has no one to fill them anymore, or simply can't be used to perform the tasks they once had so much flare for in life. When someone dies and is torn from your life I think the hardest thing to face afterwards are the empty shoes. They are a reminder of all things great and small come and gone. All of a sudden many memories flood your mind as you gaze upon those empty shoes. Shoes are one of few things that tell us that a person lived and breathed, walked and talked, laughed and cried, ran and skipped.

Whatever loss a person has faced whether it be a death, a spouse leaving, an abducted child, an abandoned child, a child leaving home for college, or someone such as in my husband's case who has suffered a life changing disability which has caused him to completely surrender the tasks, duties, and joy of living that can totally leave him feeling desolate. It is normal to feel a certain amount of anger, confusion, bitterness, fear and uncertainty and abandonment in the situation. We are flooded sometimes with so much emotion that we cannot see clearly.

For instance, I was awakened in the middle of the night because my husband was ill. I felt so much pity for him and helplessness knowing that I could not do anything to make his disability change or to make him feel better. As I sat on the edge of our bed waiting for him to return from our master bathroom, I saw his sneakers on the floor next to the side of the bed. Even though my husband can wear his sneakers and walk around, I still saw those sneakers as Lifeless Shoes. Something snapped in me at that moment and I began to see things so differently.

When my husband broke his back, we really thought that after surgery and proper recovery time he would heal and make a full recovery. He was only thirty years old when he broke his back. I remembered him being so full of life. He worked sixty plus hours at his full time job and had even done a part time job on the side for a while. He was up at three o'clock in the morning to start his day and was home again at five in the afternoon. In the course of a day he had to manage the yard, vehicles, snow blowing or shoveling in the winter, and just being a dad and husband. He also held down three or four ministries in our church. He never sat still even though he was often exhausted from having had so much to do. He wrestled with the boys, fished, and kept himself in very good shape.

As I sat staring into his empty sneakers that night, I was overcome with such emotion realizing that those shoes were not used for those things anymore. It pained me greatly to see at the time my thirty year old husband become so inactive and live every moment of his life in extreme pain. Some days I ached to have him pick me up and give me a twirl in his arms. I ached for my children to be able to wrestle dad and not be afraid that they will hurt his back more. I longed for the days when we took a nice vacation and never dreamed of worrying about dad not being able to handle taking the trip because of his back. So many things in our life changed the day his back broke. It did not just affect my husband and me. It affected all three of our children as well.

The things that I began seeing differently were the importance that I had been putting on all the wrong things. Bad hair days, a rough day teaching school, instructing a piano student who just did not want to play, coping with kids fighting, worrying about not having enough money, being angry that our life had changed for what seemed the worst and the list goes on. The Lord showed me with those empty shoes that night to focus on the things that mattered. He helped me to let the things go in a day that upset me and was causing me to lash out at the things and loved ones that mattered most.

Whatever kind of loss you are dealing with, it is so easy to look at those empty shoes and remember and long for things to be the way they used to be. What I have learned in doing so is this. Our eyes eventually are taken off of the Lord. Then we become depressed.

"That is why, for Christ's sake, I delight in weaknesses, in insults, in hardships, in persecutions, in difficulties. For when I am weak, then I am strong" (2 Corinthians 12:10).

God takes these things that hurt us and perfects us in every way. That is why struggles are so painful. Every area of your character is being pruned and then polished. You will get through it at some point, maybe not as quickly as you may wish, but you will be stronger when it is through. Remember the scripture we learned earlier.

"And we know that in all things God works for the good of those who love him, who have been called according to his purpose" (Romans 8: 28).

I am not perfect. I will still see those empty, lifeless shoes, but instead, I will try to see them as being filled by a man that can still feel our hugs and kisses and that can give them in return. I will see a man called of God and for some reason called to suffer for some time. It is okay with me not to know why, but just to rest in the Lord and believe there will come a day when my husband will be restored. Even if my husband were never to be restored to his whole self, we will not abandon what God has called us to do. Paul says this,

"For to me, to live is Christ and to die is gain" (Philippians 1:21).

Even though Paul is talking of a physical death here, I cannot help but to feel my husband and I die to the things he cannot do and the life we want to live but cannot fulfill. And it is all right because what we really want is to walk where God wants us to be. This is where it is for now. We must walk in the valley to experience the mountaintop.

Chapter Thirteen

In His Own Words...

Much of this book speaks about what it is like living with someone who is a chronic pain sufferer. You have heard mostly from my point of view how this is affecting our family. What you have not heard is how this is affecting the man that lives with this everyday. This is why I've entitled this chapter, *In His Own Words*. This is his story, his pain; his nightmare...

According to him, "When I broke my back and was unable to live the kind of life I once lived, it was discouraging. I felt and still do feel that I have been stripped of my manhood." In the world's eyes and especially his, he emphasizes, "A man is considered and looked upon to be strong and to be a leader. I feel I am neither." It is true that a lot of the physical strength he did have at one point in time is no longer there. There are times he will fix minor things around the house or on our vehicles however, even in these small tasks, he voices his discomforts and remarks how the simple things he used to take for granted are not so simple anymore. He reminisces, "I had a good job before I broke my back. I held a lot of responsibility; I did a good job. I worked my way up until I was offered the highest paying route and was offered the opportunity to train other drivers when there were other guys that had worked there longer than I." When Russ was moved to another route for any reason or if someone would fill in for him for a day he notes, "My clients would ask for me, and they were very disappointed if they were told I would not return. I enjoyed the business relationships that I had made; the friendships, and the sense of achievement knowing people were satisfied with my work and just knowing I was being a good provider for my family. The positive reactions from my clients spoke louder than anything about how I strived to do my work unto the Lord and not for man. Now I just don't feel needed anymore," he says.

I have always heard that men get their self-esteem from their work, and that women get their self-esteem from their husbands. We have found this to be so true. He no longer gets those little self-esteem boosters because he doesn't work anymore, and I find that sometimes I lack confidence because our roles have changed so much. "Going from a thirteen hour a day career to becoming virtually inactive all day is difficult to swallow," he says. This is not at all the only thing however that has been taken away from him.

When we sat down to put all of his thoughts together, we really had to think hard about some of the changes that he has had to make in his life. Some of the changes just stick right out, maybe because they are the ones most noticeable to us or maybe just because they bother us the most. For example, he states, "I used to love to putter in the shed, around the house, or around the yard after work whenever I had time. This was a stress reliever. Not only was there daily maintenance on vehicles and in the house that I never thought twice about tackling, but there were things that I just loved to do such as fishing with my boys, or playing football and wrestling them before bedtime, or playing out with the band two or three nights out of the week." Now the lack of those things is obvious to us and to all that know him. Those are things his body just does not allow him to do. Those that live with a disability find their lives crippled in many ways that go unseen by all the others around.

The extremely simple things in life can become such a chore. He emphasizes, "Because of the extreme pain I live with all day and night, and the fact that the flexibility of my back has greatly decreased, I can't even brush my teeth like a "normal" person anymore. In order to keep my back perfectly straight, I have to get into a squat position at the sink and hope that my spit will make it anywhere but on my shoes. My shaving has changed greatly due to the fact that I can't lean and get close to the mirror to see what I am doing." He proceeded to tell me of very private and embarrassing issues that deal with going to the bathroom and our intimacy as husband and wife that have not been left untouched by this condition. He continues, "I cannot sit or stand for any longer than a fifteen minute stretch at a time. I absolutely need a cushioned chair, or a recliner to sit in to keep my back from becoming inflamed over and over. As a matter of fact, for about a year after my surgery, I had to sit in a thick, cushioned porch chair at the dinner table just so I could EAT in some comfort." He had used a cane at times for when we were in the stores because the cement floors do a number on his back. He also has an action floatation cushion to sit on in the vehicles, which helps to absorb some of the shock the back sustains during any traveling. He definitely needs his special chair for his schoolwork as he sits and studies and uses the computer.

Before the stimulator implant he had started with a tens unit strapped and hooked up to his back sending stimulation to the nerve endings to try to block the pain. He shares, "I get so sore, that I have to do my back and leg stretches three or four times a day. Every morning at about four A.M., I wake up in pain and toss and turn until the alarm screams that it is time to get up and start another day. If my wife can give me a deep massage and pound gently on my lower back with her fists, it helps to loosen me up so that I can move. Every morning I take a very hot shower and let the hot water penetrate the muscles in my back. This also loosens me up and gives me a little flexibility. Then it's time to get on the floor for the first set of stretches for the day." Throughout the course of the day I will witness him having to lie down at least a couple of times. Rest and deep massages are the only things that help him at the time of discomfort. When he sits on a couch, he always has to sit on the corner end in order to maintain good posture and to give the stability he needs for a piece of furniture that is not very firm. I think this paints a pretty good picture of the things you do not see that we suffer silently with everyday of our lives.

There are definitely things on the outside that are very visible and which alert even a stranger that he lives in great pain. For example: when he moves from one position to another, he is quite stiff, or perhaps moves quite slowly, and usually there is a moan or two in there as well. Due to the medicines once again, we were always looking for things he had loss or misplaced, arguing over details that he could not recall, or messages he would forget to give me. We observed as his body would shake out of control, sweat profusely, and his eyes and nose would run uncontrollably. He would also have sneezing fits and his heart would beat sporadically as well as give him chest pain.

But perhaps the thing that concerned him the most was not being able to be active with our three boys and daughter. He states, "I have dreams that I can run again. Then reality hits me that I won't be able to wrestle the kids that night, or run and jump, or throw that football they keep asking me about. I do try throwing it, but it's definitely not like before and it really yanks on my back, and boy do I suffer for it later." Sometimes it is worth a little suffering if it means it will bring our children complete joy.

Since we do not go for long vacations, or hiking trips, we try to be creative in finding things we can do as a family or that daddy can do with the kids. For instance, we bought the boys pellet rifles for Christmas so that they can go out with dad to shoot some cans for a few minutes. We invest what extra money we do have into musical instruments for the kids AND dad, since that is also one other thing he can do with us and is ultimately the desire of his heart, to play for the Lord. I'm glad we have done that because there has been a very strong bond between him and the boys ever since. That helps dispel any fear of the kids growing up disappointed that dad couldn't or wasn't like everyone else's dad.

He has been home more even though now he is attending college in order to retrain for some other type of living. In some ways, it has been a blessing to have him home more than the average dad. One, he is able to discipline the children more than if he had still been working thirteen hour days. Two, he can love them and be apart of their lives more, and we have so many more opportunities to spiritually feed them. The best thing so far that has come out of all of this is the spiritual growth in our children. It is hard to watch your children aching to do something with daddy when daddy's body just can't do it. I watched at the time our three year old little girl, now seven, with deep expressions of concern as daddy put in another bad day with his back. It cuts us like a knife, that she may never know her daddy the way he used to be. He gets choked up and says, "Little girls are supposed to grow up seeing daddies be tough and strong. What does this tell her when she sees that I am not like most other dads? I'm concerned that she will not know what to look for in a man whether it is the masculine, physical features, or simply in the strength and security he is supposed to give her."

Knowing what it was like growing up as a boy, and all the taunting from other boys about your size and masculinity, it hits closer to home when he thinks of his boys, especially now that our oldest boy is now sixteen, and our second boy is now eleven. The, "my dad can beat up your dad" theory sticks out in his mind. "I'm worried about how my disability is affecting our boys. What goes through their minds when they see I am constantly in pain and continue to say I can't do this or that? Will they become over confident because they have had to take on more responsibilities than the average child? Will they then feel no need to turn to God or anyone else for help? Will they swing the other way and be inferior because they see me in a weakened state all of the time? They see I have to depend on everyone... Will they? Are my boys going to be wimps in sports or when there is an altercation with a peer?" These are all questions that concern him deeply and that I was never aware of.

When the medical route has been exhausted and days go by with no changes in pain, doubt and fear can become your best friends. For anyone who is a chronic pain sufferer, or lives with someone who is, I think it's easy to begin to put your hope in the doctors and medicine. Sometimes you feel God has failed you because you still wait for your miracle. When God of all people has chosen not to answer you, it's frantic at times, and doctors, procedures, and new medicines seem like your only hope. I remembered traveling to endless doctor appointments just hoping that someone in the medical field would tell us, "Good news, we have seen cases just like yours and we want to inform you that probably somewhere in the next couple of months, you will be on the road to recovery." We left discouraged however, because even in the medical field people were baffled at the end of our appointment. More fear than ever can seep in when you see professionals with puzzled looks on their faces.

There is nothing more frustrating than being at a very busy clinic only to be seen by the nurse practitioner that's scheduled to work that day. Many appointments came and went when we would see person after person who had no clue who we were, let alone the history of his medical condition. There were people doing surgical procedures on my husband that did them in a manner that proved not to have been in the most proficient form or technique. By the time the fifth resident had seen him and had completed medical procedures on him, they still had no clue of his history, the procedures he had experienced, or his prognosis. It's easy to feel like someone's guinea pig.

It's not as difficult to have faith and believe when a trial is short lived. Doubt in these cases is usually fleeting. When the table is turned and your trial does not seem to dissipate, or the furnace is cranked as hot as it can be, then the doubt comes in like the tide, crashing in on the rock on which you stand. It becomes difficult to stand against the tide crashing in or the strong winds that bend you over, but Jesus said all we need is the faith of a little mustard seed. If you ever have the opportunity to look at a mustard seed, you will be able to better understand why Jesus used that analogy. All He requires is a "tiny" bit of faith. A mustard seed is so small, yet what an enormous, strong plant it produces. That is what Jesus is telling us through this, that if we can just hold on, we will accrue more and more faith, faith strong enough that we could say to this mountain, "Be ye removed!"

"Therefore, since we have been justified through faith, we have peace with God through our Lord Jesus Christ, through whom we have gained access by faith into this grace in which we now stand. And we rejoice in the hope of the glory of God. Not only so, but we also rejoice in our sufferings, because we know that suffering produces perseverance; perseverance, character; and character, hope. And hope does not disappoint us, because God has poured out his love into our hearts by the Holy Spirit, whom he has given us," (Romans 5:3-5).

You will overcome, maybe not in the way you anticipate, but God never wastes an opportunity to turn to good, things that were intended to harm. Your trials will someday be turned to gold. You will become stronger, wiser, more cautious, and eager than ever to help the next one who follows in your shoes. The challenge is to never give up your faith. The victory is when you walk out smoky, and dusty but not burned. Then you have stood the test and can know His good and perfect will.

"It's not a question of whether or not He can heal me because I know God can do anything; I just 'DOUBT' that He will do it for me. My father began having trouble with his eyes and eventually became legally blind, forcing him out of the work force as well. Shortly thereafter, he too began feeling the call of God upon him. Now, many years later my father's eyesight has worsen, leaving him with one glass eye and one eye that is constantly giving him trouble. I can't help thinking that I will be just like my dad. Serve God wholeheartedly, only to never fully receive a healing, just continue to get worse. It's discouraging for sure. I am in more pain more times than not, when I am ministering because it requires more of me. To stand or sit and play guitar, or to fill in and preach for my father all test my physical endurance. I often am in great pain for days following."

If doubt wasn't enough to have to battle, the worse thing has to be what he thinks people think of him. "I wonder what people think or say about me behind my back. Do my close friends, people in my family, or church family think I'm faking?" We have some close friends who have empty stares on their faces whenever the topic of his back comes up. They simply have no clue to the degree of our suffering. That has just killed us. To go from having something in common with friends and then to be called to a place of suffering where no one, not even our closest family member will ever understand unless he or she has walked the same road, is just simply devastating.

When your whole world changes because of a physical suffering, spiritual things begin to happen when you walk with the Lord. It places you on a different plane from the rest of the people. Not that you are above anyone else, but you will know the Father in a way that your friends will not, if ever. That doesn't mean that they do not have a close walk with the Lord, it just means the deeper you are taken into the water, the more you depend on God, and come to know Him differently. There is one thing for sure though, if there comes a time when our friends go deep into the water, we will be there coaching them on. Why? Because other than family or a few church members, we did not have an entourage of friends spurring us on in our faith, therefore we felt alone most of the time. There were a few people in church that would offer to care for the children or we knew were being prayer warriors for us. These were people we never expected would reach out to us. The ones we thought would, called maybe once or twice a year, but basically showed no concern as to what we were up against, and never even asked. That throws some salt into an open wound. When days drag on with no changes in sight, it can become more and more difficult to wait for God's plan to manifest. I want to walk out of this, and to see this come full circle. I want to look back and see why we went through all of this and what came out of it all. It seems like forever. This scripture gives us hope and can be yours too.

"...being confident of this, that he who began a good work in you will carry it on to completion until the day of Christ Jesus" (Philippians 1:6).

After reading this scripture, I have come to the realization that if this problem with my husband's back, struggles with depression and anger did not exist, or even if his back gets better in the future, that there most definitely would be some other trial in its place that would be causing us to grow again or even more than the last time. Until the Lord comes back for us, we are on a journey in which we are to win souls for Christ. Yet we must do this as we face adversities and wrestle with doubt. When the rungs of your ladder start to break and you are hanging by one arm, do not look at what surrounds you, or at what you face beneath you, for then you will surely fall. Instead, look heaven bound; reach for the hand of the Father with the hand that broke free from its grasp. When your eyes are focused above, everything else begins to look small in comparison.

Whatever the trial, whatever wounds you, learn from them, grow from them, and make the most of them. Know that God has a higher purpose for you, and that all of the struggles we face are causing us to really become stronger in the end, as long as we do not let ourselves be defeated by them. Rise to the occasion; be like Esther, "For such a time as this." Shake off the dust, and keep working at your faith until you draw your last breath. Choose to find joy, choose to help someone else, choose life don't choose to be bound like I did for so many years.

Even though we have not seen a complete manifestation of a miraculous healing in Russ's back, miracles do envelope us each day. The sound of our children's voices, the warmth of one another's embraces, the smell of a new strong, healthy baby; the sight of a broken man serving God wholeheartedly, and the taste of his lips to mine. A secret code that did not come unsealed despite what we faced and yet it still remains a code that will never be broken.

www.ingramcontent.com/pod-product-compliance
Lightning Source LLC
Chambersburg PA
CBHW051759040426
42446CB00007B/444